Moved by
the Spirit

God's Power at Work
in His People

Moved by the Spirit

God's Power at Work in His People

Kevin Perrotta

the WORD
among us®
press

The Word Among Us Press
9639 Doctor Perry Road
Ijamsville, Maryland 21754
www.wordamongus.org

14 13 12 11 10   2 3 4 5 6

ISBN: 978-1-59325-114-7

Nihil Obstat: The Rev. Michael Morgan, Chancellor
Censor Librorum
January 9, 2009
Imprimatur: +Most Rev. Victor Galeone, Bishop of St. Augustine
January 9, 2009

Cover and text design by David Crosson

Made and printed in the United States of America

Library of Congress Cataloging-in-Publication Data
Perrotta, Kevin.
Moved by the Spirit : God's power at work in his people / Kevin Perrotta.
p. cm.
ISBN 978-1-59325-114-7
1. Holy Spirit--Biblical teaching. 2. Holy Spirit--Textbooks. I. Title.

BS2545.H62P47 2009
248.4'82--dc22
2008047023

Contents

Welcome to
The Word Among Us
Keys to the Bible

Have you ever lost your keys? Everyone seems to have at least one "lost keys" story to tell. Maybe you had to break a window of your house or wait for the auto club to let you into your car. Whatever you had to do probably cost you—in time, energy, money, or all three. Keys are definitely important items to have on hand!

The guides in The Word Among Us Keys to the Bible series are meant to provide you with a handy set of keys that can "unlock" the treasures of the Scriptures for you. Scripture is God's living word. Within its pages we meet the Lord. So as we study and meditate on Scripture and unlock its many treasures, we discover the riches it contains—and in the process, we grow in intimacy with God.

Since 1982 *The Word Among Us* magazine has helped Catholics develop a deeper relationship with the Lord through daily meditations that bring the Scriptures to life. More than ever, Catholics today desire to read and pray with the Scriptures, and many have begun to form small faith-sharing groups to explore the Bible together.

We designed the Keys to the Bible series after conducting a survey among our magazine readers to learn what they wanted in a Catholic Bible study. We found that they were looking for easy-to-understand, faith-filled materials that approach Scripture from a clearly Catholic perspective. Moreover, they wanted a Bible study that shows them how they can apply what they learn from Scripture to their everyday lives. They also asked for sessions that they can complete in an hour or two.

Our goal was to design a simple, easy-to-use Bible study guide that is also challenging and thought provoking. We hope that this guide fulfills those admittedly ambitious goals. We are confident, however, that taking the time to go through this guide—whether by yourself, with a friend, or in a small group—will be a worthwhile endeavor that will bear fruit in your life.

How to Use the Guides in This Series

The study guides in the Keys to the Bible series are divided into six sessions that each deal with a particular aspect of the topic. Before starting the first session, take the time to read the introduction, which sets the stage for the sessions that follow.

Whether you use this guide for personal reflection and study, as part of a faith-sharing group, or as an aid in your prayer time, be sure to begin each session with prayer. Ask God to open his word to you and to speak to you personally. Read each Scripture passage slowly and carefully. Then, take as much time as you need to meditate on the passage and pursue any thoughts it brings to mind. When you are ready, move on to the accompanying commentary, which offers various insights into the text.

Two sets of questions are included in each session to help you "mine" the Scripture passage and discover its relevance to your life. Those under the heading "Understand!" focus on the text itself and help you grasp what it means. Occasionally a question allows for a variety of answers and is meant to help you explore the passage from several angles. "Grow!" questions are intended to elicit a personal response by helping you examine your life in light of the values and truths that you uncover through your study of the Scripture passage and its setting. Under the headings "Reflect!" and "Act!" we offer suggestions to help you respond concretely to the challenges posed by the passage.

Finally, pertinent quotations from the Fathers of the Church as well as insights from contemporary writers appear throughout each session. Coupled with relevant selections from the *Catechism of the Catholic Church* and information about the history, geography, and culture of first-century Palestine, these selections (called

"In the Spotlight") add new layers of understanding and insight to your study.

As is true with any learning resource, you will benefit the most from this study by writing your answers to the questions in the spaces provided. The simple act of writing can help you formulate your thoughts more clearly—and will also give you a record of your reflections and spiritual growth that you can return to in the future to see how much God has accomplished in your life. End your reading or study with a prayer thanking God for what you have learned—and ask the Holy Spirit to guide you in living out the call you have been given as a Christian in the world today.

Although the Scripture passages to be studied and the related verses for your reflection are printed in full in each guide (from the Revised Standard Version: Catholic Edition), you will find it helpful to have a Bible on hand for looking up other passages and cross-references or for comparing different translations.

The format of the guides in The Word Among Us Keys to the Bible series is especially well suited for use in small groups. Some recommendations and practical tips for using this guide in a Bible discussion group are offered on pages 110–113.

We hope that this guide will unlock the meaning of the Scriptures for you and enable you to see the Spirit at work—in you and in the world today.

The Word Among Us Press

Introduction
More of the Holy Spirit

Would you like to be a better person—still yourself, but a better, improved version of yourself? Well, there's good news. This is what God wants for you, and he has a plan for bringing it about.

God's plan is not something you need to qualify for, and you don't have to pay for it, either. God will make the needed renovations. You simply need to acknowledge that this really is what you need and give God a free hand to proceed according to his plan.

You do have to share in the work. But God will supply all the materials and will carry out the project from start to finish.

The personal transformation is like totally remodeling your house. You could think of it as an extreme personal makeover.

Sounds promising? Scary? Too good to be true? However it sounds, it is real. It is, in fact, the gospel of Jesus Christ. The gospel—the word means "good news"—that Jesus proclaimed was this: "The kingdom of God is at hand; repent" (Mark 1:15). "The kingdom of God" means God's loving dominion over our entire lives. To "repent" is to admit that you need a total makeover.

God's dominion over our lives has a far-in-the-future phase, when Jesus returns and brings God's dominion over everything and everybody in a complete way. The kingdom also has a present phase—God reigning over us and within us, at the core of our being, by his Holy Spirit.

Jesus pointed to the coming of the Spirit as the goal of his ministry. Jesus told his disciples that his departure, at the conclusion of his work on earth, would be to their benefit—hard as that might be for them to accept—because through his departure, the Holy Spirit would come to them (see John 16:7). Thus, in Jesus' view, this is the outcome of his teaching, death, and resurrection: the way is now open for the Holy Spirit to come to us (see John 20:19-23).

St. Seraphim of Sarov, a Russian monk of the nineteenth century, declared that the whole purpose of the Christian life is to get more of the Holy Spirit—to have the Spirit at work in us, making the renovations that God has in mind. He was just saying in a particularly striking way what many saints east and west have said in one way or another for centuries.

Questions about the Spirit

Who is this Holy Spirit? And what exactly does he come to do in our lives? Inquiring into the Spirit takes us to the heart of the mystery of God—perhaps we should say, *mysteries.*

God is infinitely mysterious to us, simply because he is the one who brought us and everything else into existence. How can we understand the one who always is and who creates from nothing? Yet even more mysterious is the inner life of God. In God, the Father eternally begets the Son and breathes forth the Holy Spirit. Thus God is three divine Persons, existing in total self-giving and receiving as begetter and begotten, breather and breathed-forth, Son and Spirit. The three Persons are joined in such profound love for each other that their threeness never jeopardizes their oneness and their oneness never blurs the distinctive love that each has for the others.

Of the three Persons, the Spirit seems to be the most difficult for us to bring into focus in our minds. Since God as God is spirit—there is nothing material about him—what does it mean to call the third Person "the Spirit"? Difficult question! We could say that the Holy Spirit is all the love and power and wisdom and goodness of God in person. But that hardly clears up the mystery. (See the helpful presentation on the Trinity and the Holy Spirit in the *Catechism of the Catholic Church*: sections 232–267; 683–701.)

The mystery of the one God being a community of Persons is unfathomable. Yet the reality of it touches our lives in a very direct way. God has created us in a likeness to himself. So we can answer the question "Who am I?" only by reference to the mystery of God as a community of Persons in total love, for we are created to mirror—and enter into—their community of love.

If we think this over, we may become conscious of how far we have diverged from our basic design. Created to be like God and with God, we have chosen to go other ways. The good news is that God has made available everything necessary for radical transformation. He has sent his Son to become one of us—Jesus of Nazareth. By Jesus' death, God has vanquished the powers of sin and death that threaten to destroy us and has reconciled us to himself. In addition, God has sent his Spirit to all who are united with his Son through faith and baptism (see John 3:16; 14:15-31; Romans 5:1-11; 8:1-27). The Holy Spirit now comes to us as the architect and chief contractor of the extreme personal makeover we need. He will enable us to take our place in the relationship of total self-giving love in the community of the Father, the Son, and the Spirit.

With such a radical goal, the Spirit comes to carry out a renovation of our lives that goes beyond the refurbishing we might come up with ourselves. I might like to be a wealthy and renowned writer, but God has something bigger and better in mind; he wants me to be a great saint. I might like a process of personal change that gives me enough peace to enjoy life without anxieties—something less than an *extreme* personal makeover. But the Holy Spirit isn't interested in such limited outcomes. As the divine building contractor, the Spirit does not aim at producing little condo units suitable for private pleasures. He wants to make us into spacious homes, equipped for welcoming and serving people with all kinds of needs.

Our Plan in This Book

In this book, we are going to focus on the vitally important mystery of the Holy Spirit's action in our lives. What does the Spirit come to do in us? How can we experience his presence and cooperate with him? What will happen to us if we do?

The Bible is filled with revelation about the Spirit. We see hints of him at the beginning (see Genesis 1:2), and he appears at the end (see Revelation 22:17). The Old Testament speaks of the Spirit as inspiring, instructing, and empowering. In New Testament texts, Jesus and the early leaders of the Church have a great deal to say about the Holy Spirit. Out of all this varied material, we will read just six passages. But they will give us a wealth of insight and will point us toward many ways that we can open ourselves to the action of the Spirit.

We begin with two gospel readings that show us the Spirit in those who welcomed Jesus' birth, especially his mother, Mary; a relative of hers, Elizabeth; and two elderly residents of Jerusalem, Simeon and Anna. Our third reading focuses on Jesus himself and what he said about the Spirit's presence within him. Then we look at a few people who experienced the power of the Spirit after Jesus' death, resurrection, and return to the Father—especially a man named Philip and a woman named Tabitha.

As you read about these people, try to keep your eyes on the Spirit. Of course, the Spirit is not visible in any of the events, because the Spirit is always invisible. Trying to keep your eyes on the Spirit as he moves in people's lives is like watching a basketball game on TV in which a computer graphics program has erased the ball: you can tell where the ball is and what's happening to it only by watching the players as they move around the court. That might be difficult at first, but you would get good at it with practice. So also with keeping your eyes on the Holy Spirit—both in Scripture and in the world today.

In the first five sessions of Moved by the Spirit, we will read passages from a single author, St. Luke. The first three sessions are from the gospel that bears his name. Sessions Four and Five are from Luke's other book, the Acts of the Apostles. Since all five of these passages are narratives—stories—they report on the Spirit's activity but do not discuss or explain it. It will be up to us as we read to ask questions about the Spirit's action and try to grasp the message for our own lives. The commentary and questions in each weekly session will help.

Our final reading, from St. Paul's Second Letter to the Corinthians, is just the opposite kind of treatment. Instead of a story, Paul gives us instruction. He speaks especially about the interplay between our weaknesses and sufferings on the one hand and the power and encouragement of the Spirit on the other. Paul brings us to the heart of the Spirit's extreme personal renovation project in our lives.

As you read, take time to think, question, reflect, and pray. Then pick up a hammer, and join in with whatever project the Spirit is currently working on in you.

Kevin Perrotta

Mothers and Sons

Luke 1:39-48, 56

³⁹In those days Mary arose and went with haste into the hill country, to a city of Judah, ⁴⁰and she entered the house of Zechariah and greeted Elizabeth. ⁴¹And when Elizabeth heard the greeting of Mary, the babe leaped in her womb; and Elizabeth was filled with the Holy Spirit ⁴²and she exclaimed with a loud cry, "Blessed are you among women, and blessed is the fruit of your womb! ⁴³And why is this granted me, that the mother of my Lord should come to me? ⁴⁴For behold, when the voice of your greeting came to my ears, the babe in my womb leaped for joy. ⁴⁵And blessed is she who believed that there would be a fulfillment of what was spoken to her from the Lord." ⁴⁶And Mary said,

"My soul magnifies the Lord,
⁴⁷and my spirit rejoices in God my Savior,
⁴⁸for he has regarded the low estate of his
handmaiden. . . ."
⁵⁶And Mary remained with her about three months, and returned to her home.

> **H**ail, thou that art the throne of the King:
> Hail, thou who dost hold Him who holdeth all.
> Hail, thou through whom the creation is made new:
> Hail, thou through whom the Creator becomes a newborn child.
> —**Byzantine Hymn**

Elizabeth and her husband, Zechariah, were an elderly and deeply religious Jewish couple. Some months before the incident in our reading, an angel had very unexpectedly announced to Zechariah that Elizabeth, who had never borne a child, was going to be a mother. The boy she would bear, the angel declared, would be "great before the Lord" (Luke 1:15)—a messenger sent by God to urge people to turn back to him.

A few months later, the same angel, Gabriel, appeared to a very young Jewish woman named Mary. Gabriel told Mary that she would become pregnant by the power of the Holy Spirit, without sexual relations with a man. Her child would be "great" indeed, for he would be the Son of God. Mary responded that she was willing to cooperate with this unusual divine plan: "Let it be to me according to your word" (Luke 1:38).

During their conversation, the angel informed Mary that Elizabeth—who was a relative of hers—had become pregnant. As soon as the angel departed, Mary set out to visit Elizabeth. As our reading begins, Mary is arriving at Elizabeth's house.

We may suppose that Mary gives Elizabeth a customary greeting—something like "Hello, Auntie Elizabeth." But her greeting elicits a surprising response. Elizabeth's child jumps in her womb, and Elizabeth bursts out in a loud cry. "Blessed are you among women!" she yells out to her undoubtedly astonished visitor.

This flurry of activity reflects the presence of the Holy Spirit, who has instantaneously given Elizabeth an insight into the identity of the child Mary is carrying: he is the Lord! In a rush of words inspired by the Spirit, Elizabeth rejoices, proclaims what is happening, describes her experience of inspiration, and offers Mary encouragement. A medieval English monk named Bede wrote that Elizabeth "couldn't praise the Lord with a moderate voice. Being filled with the Holy Spirit, she was on fire. She rejoiced that the Lord had come!"

Elizabeth hears Mary's greeting with her ears; she feels the baby kicking in her womb; she grasps the meaning of Mary's visit with her mind; she shouts with a loud voice. Her whole self senses the Spirit's action and responds.

"Blessed are you among women," Elizabeth cries out to Mary (Luke 1:42)—meaning that Mary is the most blessed woman there is. God has given her the supreme blessing of becoming the mother of his Son.

And, Elizabeth adds, Mary is blessed for believing that God will do what he said he would do (see Luke 1:45). Elizabeth is congratulating Mary: "You're on the right track! Keep on trusting God!" We don't know whether Mary is feeling a need for encouragement, but Elizabeth hasn't waited to find out. She offers encouragement freely. Filled with the Spirit, she can't help but express her confidence in God.

Here we discover an important aspect of the Spirit's work. No situation is too small or too ordinary for him.

At the same time, Elizabeth recognizes her unworthiness to receive a visit from the Lord and his mother. "How does such a thing happen, that my Lord's mother has come to me?" In Elizabeth's humility, too, we can detect the presence of the Spirit.

Amazingly, Elizabeth's son, who will be named John, is also caught up in the action of the Spirit. The tiny child *in utero* is rambunctious with joy. He brings to mind a statement that Jesus will later make: "Whoever does not receive the kingdom of God like a child shall not enter it" (Luke 18:17). Little John gives us a picture of the simple, childlike reception the Spirit seeks from us.

Luke does not say so, but it goes without saying that Mary also is filled with the Spirit as she prays (sings?) a declaration of God's greatness. Her prayer expresses a deep understanding of God's mercy, faithfulness, and concern for justice. (Read her entire prayer in Luke 1:46-55.)

Fortunately for us, this episode is not just a long-ago event. The Spirit who filled Mary, Elizabeth, and little John, and then guided the gospel writer Luke, is with us, too. If we read Luke's Spirit-filled account with humility and openness to God's action—the kind of humility and openness we witness in Mary and Elizabeth—the Spirit will bring us into contact with this event and with Jesus, the hidden center of it. The Spirit urges us to share Mary's confidence that God will fulfill his words to us—his promises of forgiveness, strength, transformation, and eternal life. The Spirit invites us to enter into Elizabeth's whole-self response to Jesus' coming, and even into John's exuberance.

How does Jesus come to us today? The ways are many. He comes in Scripture and in the sacraments, especially in the celebration of the Eucharist and in holy Communion. He comes to us in unexpected inspirations of the Spirit. He comes to us, as he came to Elizabeth, in his mother, who continues to play a vital role in the Church as mother of the Lord and our mother, too.

If anyone had been searching for God's activity in the world on the day Mary arrived at Elizabeth's house, I doubt that they would have looked there. In those days, men were almost exclusively responsible for public affairs. Why would anyone pay attention to the talk of two women? And wouldn't God be more likely to make himself known in public, in the Temple in Jerusalem, than in a private home? To an outside observer, Mary's visit to Elizabeth might seem insignificant.

Yet here we discover an important aspect of the Spirit's work. No situation is too small or too ordinary for him. The Spirit of God is present with us in the everyday. A Byzantine hymn joyfully declares to him: "You are everywhere present and fill all things!"

Understand!

1. Why do you think Mary went to visit Elizabeth? Why did she stay on for three months? What effect do you think her visit might have had on Elizabeth? On Zechariah? On Mary herself?

_____

_____

_____

_____

_____

_____

2. Elizabeth (Luke 1:43) and Mary (1:46) make humble responses to God's action. What is humility? Why is it important in responding to the Holy Spirit?

_____

_____

_____

_____

_____

_____

3. Mary "magnifies the Lord" (Luke 1:46), that is, she declares the Lord's greatness. What does it mean to declare God's greatness? Why should we declare God's greatness?

_____

_____

_____

_____

_____

_____

4. Luke tells us how Elizabeth experienced Mary, not how Mary experienced Elizabeth. What do you think Mary's thoughts might have been in her encounter with Elizabeth?

_____

_____

_____

_____

_____

_____

5. What insight does this story give us into children in the womb?

_____

_____

_____

_____

_____

▶ In the Spotlight
Mary Stayed On

Why did Mary remain with Elizabeth for three months? An early Christian scholar named Origen (c. 185–c. 254) suggested that the answer had to do with Elizabeth's son, the future St. John the Baptist. Origen wrote:

From Mary's merely coming to Elizabeth and greeting her, "the infant leaped with joy" and "Elizabeth, filled with the Spirit, prophesied." If, in a single hour, John experienced such development, it is left to us to deduce how much he advanced during Mary's three-month stay with Elizabeth. If the infant jumped with joy and Elizabeth was filled with the Holy Spirit in a single minute, it is inconceivable that they would make no further progress by living in the presence of the mother of the Lord and of the savior himself for three months. Rather, during those three months, while John was still in his mother's womb, he was trained—we might even say, he was anointed like a wrestler in the arena—in preparation for the spiritual combat that lay ahead.

—Origen, *Homilies on St. Luke*

Grow!

1. Mary believed that God would fulfill his word to her (Luke 1:45). In what situation in your life do you find it difficult to trust in God's faithfulness to you? What steps could you take to grow in trust in God in that situation?

_____

_____

_____

_____

_____

_____

_____

2. Do you, like Elizabeth, overflow with confidence in God (Luke 1:45)? Do you encourage others to have faith in God? Do you ask the Holy Spirit to make you an agent of his encouragement to others? Pick out someone you know to whom you could offer encouragement. How will you encourage them?

_____

_____

_____

_____

_____

_____

3. The Spirit gave Elizabeth a sudden awareness of God's action. Have you ever experienced this kind of grace? (Possible examples: Recognizing that a difficult situation is a trial allowed by God for a purpose. Seeing another person as loved by God. Feeling assured that a situation is in God's care.) How could you become more open to the Spirit's inspirations?

_____

_____

_____

_____

_____

_____

4. When you hear other people's good news or descriptions of their experiences of God, do you respond, like Elizabeth, with joy? Or is your response tinged with envy? What's wrong with envy? How could you become more like Elizabeth?

_____

_____

_____

_____

_____

_____

_____

5. How is praise a declaration of God's greatness? How often do you praise God in prayer? In a liturgical setting? What difference does it make when you do so?

_____

_____

_____

_____

_____

_____

▶ In the Spotlight
A Little One's Relationship with God

John exults . . . before he is born. Before his eyes can see what the world looks like, he can recognize the Lord of the world with his spirit. In this regard, I think that the prophetic phrase is appropriate: "Before I formed you in the womb I knew you,

and before you came forth from the womb I sanctified you"
(Jeremiah 1:5).
—Maximus of Turin

Reflect!

1. Picture the setting of our reading and replay the event in your mind. Be quiet for a time. What strikes you most forcefully in this incident? If something occurs to you, express your thought to God. But remember, the most important thing is to be present and attentive at the scene. Here are some aids for imagination and reflection:

—Reread the passage slowly more than once; try reading it aloud.
—Look at an icon of the Visitation.
—Meditate on the scene before the Blessed Sacrament.
—Pray a decade of the rosary on the Visitation.
—Repeat Elizabeth's words in Luke 1:43-44 over and over.

2. Read and reflect on the following passages to enrich your understanding of our reading:

Get you up to a high mountain,
   O Zion, herald of good tidings;
lift up your voice with strength,
   O Jerusalem, herald of good tidings,
   lift it up, fear not;
say to the cities of Judah,
   "Behold your God!"
Behold, the Lord GOD comes with might,
   and his arm rules for him;
behold, his reward is with him,

and his recompense before him.
He will feed his flock like a shepherd,
  he will gather the lambs in his arms,
he will gather them in his bosom,
  and gently lead those that are with young."

—Isaiah 40:9-11

Now they were bringing even infants to him that he might touch them; and when the disciples saw it, they rebuked them. But Jesus called them to him, saying, "Let the children come to me, and do not hinder them; for to such belongs the kingdom of God. Truly, I say to you, whoever does not receive the kingdom of God like a child shall not enter it."

—Luke 18:15-17

3. Compare the disciples' exuberance in response to the Spirit in our reading with that of baby John's:

When the day of Pentecost had come, they were all together in one place. And suddenly a sound came from heaven like the rush of a mighty wind, and it filled all the house where they were sitting. And there appeared to them tongues as of fire, distributed and resting on each one of them. And they were all filled with the Holy Spirit and began to speak in other tongues, as the Spirit gave them utterance.

Now there were dwelling in Jerusalem Jews, devout men from every nation under heaven. And at the sound the multitude came together, and they were bewildered, because each one heard them speaking in his own language. And they were amazed and wondered, saying, "Are not all these who are speaking Galileans? And how is it that we hear, each of us in his own native language? . . . "

And all were amazed and perplexed, saying to one another, "What does this mean?" But others mocking said, "They are filled with new wine."

But Peter, standing with the eleven, lifted up his voice and addressed them, "Men of Judea and all who dwell in Jerusalem, let this be known to you, and give ear to my words. For these men are not drunk, as you suppose, since it is only the third hour of the day; but this is what was spoken by the prophet Joel:

'And in the last days it shall be, God declares, that I will pour out my Spirit upon all flesh. . . .'"

—Acts 2:1-8, 12-17

▶ In the Spotlight
A Personal Pentecost

During Pentecost Mass in 1623, Louise de Marillac experienced an outpouring of grace that ended a period of anguish and made her vividly aware of the Spirit's power and action. From then on, says her biographer J. Calvert, she was a "disciple of the Holy Spirit" and turned to him "as toward that love which would make her worthy of the Father by making her more like the Son. Said Louise: The Holy Spirit 'fills us with pure love of God. . . . The Spirit makes us obedient to God, so that we may share the divine life.'"

St. Louise marked this anniversary for the rest of her life with a yearly Ascension-to-Pentecost retreat, prayerfully preparing to welcome more of the Spirit of love into her life.

Act!

1. Ask to experience the Holy Spirit in a deeper way. Ask him to show you one way that he is already at work in your life and is at work in the life of someone around you.
2. Ask the Spirit for the wisdom to see how to cooperate with what he is doing.
3. Cooperate!

▶ In the Spotlight
Sources of a Familiar Prayer

The first line of the Hail Mary comes from the gospel episode in which the angel Gabriel announces to Mary that she is to be the mother of the Lord: "Hail, favored one! The Lord is with you" (Luke 1:28, NAB). From our reading in this session come the next words of the prayer: "Blessed are you among women, and blessed is the fruit of your womb!" (1:42). With these words, Elizabeth celebrates God's grace in Mary's life—and that is what we do when we use Elizabeth's words in the Hail Mary.

To remember God's graciousness to Mary is to remind ourselves that *our* lives also are a grace, a marvelous gift of God, and that God's grace—the power of the Holy Spirit—is offered to us at every minute.

If, by praying the Hail Mary, we join Elizabeth in congratulating Mary for being so highly graced by God, we should also take Mary as our model for believing that God will accomplish everything that he promises us.

At Mary's visit, Elizabeth cried out in the Spirit, recognizing the child as the incarnate Lord. When we pray the Hail Mary, the Spirit guides us to reflect on the incarnation of the Son of God. In acclaiming his mother, we thank Jesus for becoming the fruit of her womb, for coming among us. Let us join with Elizabeth in welcoming and congratulating Mary—and encounter the Lord who has taken flesh in her.

The Best
for Last

Luke 2:22-38

²²And when the time came for their purification according to the law of Moses, they brought him up to Jerusalem to present him to the Lord ²³(as it is written in the law of the Lord, "Every male that opens the womb shall be called holy to the Lord") ²⁴and to offer a sacrifice according to what is said in the law of the Lord, "a pair of turtledoves, or two young pigeons." ²⁵Now there was a man in Jerusalem, whose name was Simeon, and this man was righteous and devout, looking for the consolation of Israel, and the Holy Spirit was upon him. ²⁶And it had been revealed to him by the Holy Spirit that he should not see death before he had seen the Lord's Christ. ²⁷And inspired by the Spirit, he came into the temple; and when the parents brought in the child Jesus, to do for him according to the custom of the law, ²⁸he took him up in his arms and blessed God and said,

> Love the Holy Spirit, dear daughters, and invoke him often, that you may obtain for yourselves and for me that blessed light, eternal, uncreated, true, vital, and immortal.
> —St. Frances Cabrini

²⁹"Lord, now lettest thou thy servant depart in peace,
according to thy word;
³⁰for mine eyes have seen thy salvation
³¹which thou hast prepared in the presence of all peoples,
³²a light for revelation to the Gentiles,
and for glory to thy people Israel."
³³And his father and his mother marveled at what was said about him; ³⁴and Simeon blessed them and said to Mary his mother,
"Behold, this child is set for the fall and rising of many
in Israel,
and for a sign that is spoken against
³⁵(and a sword will pierce through your own soul also),
that thoughts out of many hearts may be revealed."

³⁶And there was a prophetess, Anna, the daughter of Phanuel, of the tribe of Asher; she was of a great age, having lived with her husband seven years from her virginity, ³⁷and as a widow till she was eighty-four. She did not depart from the temple, worshiping with fasting and prayer night and day. ³⁸And coming up at that very hour she gave thanks to God, and spoke of him to all who were looking for the redemption of Jerusalem.

In the lapse of time since our first reading, two great events have occurred: the birth of John the Baptist and the birth of Jesus the Messiah.

Jesus' birth transforms the lives of Mary and Joseph. The one who will bring salvation to the world is now growing up as their son, living in total dependence on them! Yet Mary and Joseph continue to follow the customary patterns of Judaism. Eight days after his birth, they have Jesus circumcised. About five weeks later, they take him with them to the Temple in Jerusalem for a ceremony prescribed by the Mosaic law.

The Temple itself—a small but splendid gold-plated building—was surrounded by a courtyard of some thirty-five acres, bounded by tall colonnades. Among the people going back and forth on this plaza on the day Mary and Joseph come with Jesus is an elderly man named Simeon.

Simeon enters the Temple "in the Spirit" because that is how he lives.

Like Elizabeth, Simeon is old, but there the similarity between them ends. In the last session's reading, Elizabeth was experiencing God's action in an extraordinary way: she had become pregnant in old age. By contrast, as far as we know, nothing special is going on in Simeon's life at the moment we catch sight of him walking across the Temple plaza. As far as we can tell, he is going about his usual routine, a routine he has probably followed for many years, which takes him into the Temple each day to pray.

Our translation says that Simeon comes into the Temple "inspired by the Spirit" (Luke 2:27), which suggests that the Spirit has given him a nudge to go there. The original Greek, however, says merely that he comes "in the Spirit." Perhaps he did not receive special guidance, but he enters the Temple "in the Spirit" because that is how he lives—in the Spirit. And because he is in the Spirit, he is where God wants him to be at this particular moment.

Luke tells us that Simeon has been looking forward to God's kingdom (see 2:26). Simeon is not just hoping that God's kingdom will come someday. He is looking for it to come in his lifetime, on the basis of a promise the Spirit has made to him.

As the old man meets Mary and Joseph on the Temple plaza, the Spirit opens his eyes to the identity of the child they are carrying. Moved by the Spirit, Simeon takes Jesus in his arms and praises God for him. This child, Simeon declares, will reveal God to all peoples. Simeon is not the only elderly person on the Temple plaza at that moment. A very old person, Anna, is there (the Greek may be interpreted to mean that she is more than a hundred years old). Coming up to the foursome on the plaza at just this moment—another meeting clearly arranged by the Spirit—she, too, is guided by the Spirit to recognize the infant Jesus for who he is.

If we place this incident next to last session's reading, a pattern emerges. In both cases, the Spirit guides people to recognize Jesus' presence and to grasp that he is Lord and Savior.

Luke's description of Simeon and Anna as prayerful and devout people brings out a further point about the Spirit's activity. These two elderly people had been prepared for the Spirit's action this day by living with the Spirit throughout their lives. Nourished by constant prayer and participation in the liturgy of the Temple, they lived consciously in God's presence. When he wished to reveal something to them, they were paying attention.

We may well suppose that both Simeon and Anna had been following established personal routines for many years, and we all know how routines can dull our sensitivities. Yet because their routines were centered on God in prayer, these two people were ready to feel the Spirit's movement on the great day when the infant Lord came into the Temple.

The setting of this scene is more impressive than Elizabeth's house. The gilded Temple, flashing in the sun, surrounded by its magnificent plaza, was one of the wonders of the ancient world. Moreover, it was a holy place. Yet the Spirit's action in the ordinary, which we saw in our last session's reading, continues here, too. The setting is splendid, but the people do not attract attention. Simeon is not one of the revered teachers learnedly discussing the Mosaic law at the entrance to the Temple plaza. He does not belong to any of the prominent priestly families that administer the Temple. Anna is a seemingly insignificant person. Mary and Joseph do not bear any signs of high social status. Yet to these ordinary people, who blend anonymously into the crowd, the Spirit of God makes the Messiah known.

The Spirit is not given on the basis of worldly importance but on the basis of God's love. He comes to the very old (Anna) and the very young (the unborn John)—indeed, to everyone (see Acts 2:17-18). Especially memorable is the image of Simeon looking down at the baby Jesus with wonder and love. "I have been waiting for this child my whole life," Simeon must have thought. "Now that he has come, the people will be saved. I have reached my goal." The old man's serenity contrasts with the excited bouncing of the unborn John in Elizabeth's womb. Together, John and Simeon give us complementary pictures of the experience of the Spirit—uncontainable joy and profound peace.

Simeon is now ready to depart from this life. This, indeed, is the Spirit's goal for all of us. In every situation, in every way that he acts in us, the Spirit is moving us toward that moment when we will enter fully into the eternal kingdom of the Father and the Son and the Holy Spirit.

Understand!

1. Simeon is considered to have been an old man, although Luke does not say this explicitly. What basis does Luke give us for thinking that Simeon is old?

_____

_____

_____

_____

_____

_____

2. Luke emphasizes that the Holy Spirit was active in Simeon's life. He also tells us that Simeon was "looking for the consolation of Israel" (2:25), that is, for God's great end-time act of salvation of the human race. What does this suggest about the Spirit's action in us?

_____

_____

_____

_____

_____

_____

3. Why is Simeon content to leave this life in peace after seeing Jesus as only an infant?

_____

_____

_____

_____

_____

4. Mary and Joseph know who Jesus is. So why do they marvel at what Simeon says about him (Luke 2:33)?

_____

_____

_____

_____

_____

_____

_____

5. The Holy Spirit is mentioned in this episode only in relation to Simeon (Luke 2:25-27). How can we know that Anna also is moved by the Spirit?

_____

_____

_____

_____

_____

_____

▶ In the Spotlight
The Offering of the Poor

Luke tells us that Mary and Joseph complied with the precept of the law of Moses that called for a new mother to make an offering to God after the birth of her child. Luke specifies that the offering required was "a pair of turtledoves, or two young pigeons" (Luke 2:24). This, however, was not the *standard* offering. According to the Mosaic law, the mother was to bring a year-old lamb and either a pigeon or a turtledove (see Leviticus 12:6). But because the expense of a lamb was a burden for a poor woman, the law permitted the mother to replace the lamb with a second bird: she could bring "a pair of turtledoves, or two young pigeons." By telling us that this was Mary's offering, Luke lets us know that Mary and Joseph had limited material means. They were not destitute—in Nazareth they had a home, and Joseph worked at a trade—but they were far from being among the more affluent members of their society. Jesus grew up in a family that was relatively poor, even by the standards of the time.

Grow!

1. In this episode, Mary and Joseph are fulfilling a customary religious obligation. Anna and maybe Simeon are following their usual patterns of prayer in the Temple. In what ways can established routines of liturgy and prayer aid our relationship with the Holy Spirit? Can they also be an obstacle?

_____

_____

_____

_____

_____

_____

_____

2. In this episode, Mary, Joseph, Simeon, and Anna experience the Spirit acting in a surprising way. When have you been surprised by the Spirit? Have you ever met the Lord in an unexpected situation? What effect has this had on your life? What message does it carry for you today?

_____

_____

_____

_____

_____

_____

_____

3. Simeon and Anna are looking for God to act on behalf of his people (Luke 2:25, 38). At their advanced age, they were unlikely to benefit, so their concern is mainly for the welfare of others. The Spirit wants to make us like these two elderly people—less concerned for our own needs than for others. How can we better cooperate with the Spirit's action?

_____

_____

_____

_____

_____

_____

4. For many years Simeon and Anna sought God's saving action for his people. The Spirit was with them as they persevered in prayer. Where is God inviting you to persevere in prayer? What obstacles do you face?

_____

_____

_____

_____

_____

_____

5. The experience of the yet unborn John and the very elderly Anna suggests that the Spirit can come to us in every stage of life. Given your stage in life and your circumstances, how do you think the Holy Spirit wishes to act in you? How will you respond?

_____

_____

_____

_____

_____

_____

_____

▶ In the Spotlight
A Prediction of Sorrow

Simeon gives Mary an ominous prediction: "A sword will pierce through your own soul also" (Luke 2:35). The old man was certainly not trying to discourage her. But, guided by the Spirit, he was warning her that suffering lay ahead, as her son became "a sign that is spoken against" (2:34). This is not the only time in Luke's writings that someone is alerted by the Spirit to oncoming suffering. In the Acts of the Apostles (also authored by Luke), a prophet named Agabus warns Paul that he is going to be arrested (see Acts 21:10-14). Apparently the Lord sometimes gives us a premonition of future difficulties so that they don't take us by surprise.

What suffering of Mary's does Simeon have in mind? The greatest suffering to befall her will be the death of her son. Another level of meaning, however, lies in Simeon's image of a sword. This image sometimes refers to division or decision—being forced to choose one side or another. Jesus himself will be a sword in this sense, for he will confront people with the necessity of making a choice for or against him and his message (see Matthew 10:34; Luke 12:49-53). Simeon warns Mary that she will experience this sword also. Even though she is Jesus' mother, closeness to him will not be automatic or effortless. Like every disciple, Mary will have to *decide* to follow Jesus, and this choice will be painful when others in the family reject him.

Thus Luke portrays Mary as the model disciple of Jesus, who chose in every situation to believe in him and follow him (see also Luke 1:45; 8:21; 11:27-28).

Reflect!

1. Is there something you could add to your daily routine in order to help yourself be more attentive and available to the Spirit? Is there something you should remove?

2. Reflect on the following incident, which involves another seemingly chance encounter in the Temple. How was the Spirit at work here? What can you learn from this episode concerning how the Spirit might wish to act in your life?

> Now Peter and John were going up to the temple at the hour of prayer, the ninth hour. And a man lame from birth was being carried, whom they laid daily at that gate of the temple which is called Beautiful to ask for alms of those who entered the temple. Seeing Peter and John about to go into the temple, he asked for alms. And Peter directed his gaze at him, with John, and said, "Look at us." And he fixed his attention upon them, expecting to receive something from them. But Peter said, "I have no silver and gold, but I give you what I have; in the name of Jesus Christ of Nazareth, walk." And he took him up by the right hand and raised him up; and immediately his feet and ankles were made strong. And leaping up he stood and walked

and entered the temple with them, walking and leaping
and praising God.

—Acts 3:1-8

3. In their relationship with God, Simeon and Anna were listeners.
Reflect on this portion of Psalm 81, which is about listening to
God.

"I relieved your shoulder of the burden;
    your hands were freed from the basket.
In distress you called, and I delivered you;
    I answered you in the secret place of thunder;
    I tested you at the waters of Meribah.
Hear, O my people, while I admonish you!
    O Israel, if you would but listen to me!
There shall be no strange god among you;
    you shall not bow down to a foreign god.
I am the LORD your God,
    who brought you up out of the land of Egypt.
Open your mouth wide, and I will fill it.

"But my people did not listen to my voice;
    Israel would have none of me.
So I gave them over to their stubborn hearts,
    to follow their own counsels.
O that my people would listen to me,
    that Israel would walk in my ways!
I would soon subdue their enemies,
    and turn my hand against their foes.
Those who hate the LORD would cringe toward him,
    and their fate would last forever.
I would feed you with the finest of the wheat,
    and with honey from the rock I would satisfy you."

—Psalm 81:6-16

▶ In the Spotlight
Blessing, Blessing, and Blessing

Simeon "blessed" Mary and Joseph (Luke 2:33). He also "blessed God" (2:28). The English word (and the underlying Greek word in Luke's text) is used with obviously different meanings in these two passages. In fact, *bless* is a word whose biblical meanings face in two opposite directions.

In the first sense, bless means to give life, fertility—everything that is needed for abundant living, for success. Thus, God "blessed" our first human parents (see Genesis 1:28-29). In this sense, Simeon, as an agent of God, blesses Mary and Joseph: through his words, God gives them blessing.

In the second sense, bless means to acknowledge God as the source of blessings. Simeon blesses God by acknowledging that God has now given his supreme blessing, the Messiah. In this sense, bless means to thank and praise God for his goodness to us. Thus, we bless God in the eucharistic liturgy with the prayer "Blessed are you, Lord, God of all creation, through your goodness we have this bread to offer."

In addition, Scripture has a third sense of blessing (employing a different Greek word). In our previous reading, Elizabeth said to Mary, "Blessed is she who believed that there would be a fulfilment of what was spoken to her from the Lord" (Luke 1:45). Here, to declare blessed means to congratulate someone for the happiness that lies ahead of them. In this sense, we bless the newly married couple at their wedding: "I just know you're going to be so happy together!" Similarly, in the Sermon on the Mount, Jesus declares, "Blessed are the poor in spirit, for theirs is the kingdom of heaven" (Matthew 5:3). Jesus is saying, "You poor in spirit, rejoice, because God has great happiness in store for you!"

Act!

Simeon's longing for the "consolation of Israel" is well expressed by the first petitions of the Lord's Prayer: "Our Father who art in heaven, / Hallowed be thy name. / Thy kingdom come, / Thy will be done, / On earth as it is in heaven" (Matthew 6:9-10). The Holy Spirit is with us as we pray this prayer. Pray it repeatedly this week, asking for a greater openness to the Holy Spirit in your heart and for God's action in people's lives everywhere.

▶ In the Spotlight
Open Your Heart to the Spirit

These remarks by St. Francis de Sales (1567–1622) reflect the zoology and botany of the seventeenth century. But the point he makes about the Holy Spirit is up-to-date.

The sun's rays give both light and warmth together. Inspiration is a ray of grace bringing light and warmth to our hearts: light to show us what is good, warmth to give us the energy to go after it. All living things in this world are numbed by winter's cold; with the return of spring's warmth they come to life again—animals move more swiftly, birds fly higher with livelier song, plants gaily bud and blossom. Without inspiration the life of the soul is sluggish, impotent, useless. Once the rays of God's inspirations strike it, however, we are aware of light and life . . . our minds are enlightened, our wills are inflamed and quickened with strength to intend and fulfill whatever may lead to our salvation. . . .

The Holy Spirit is infinite light; he is the living breath of God we call inspiration. Through his Spirit God breathes into us, inspires us with the desires or intentions of his heart. The ways he has of inspiring us are past counting. . . .

Blessed are those whose hearts are ever open to God's inspiration; they will never lack what they need to live good holy lives or to perform properly the duties of their state in life.

—St. Francis de Sales, *Treatise on the Love of God*

"It's Not
Just about
You"

Luke 4:14-30

¹⁴Jesus returned in the power of the Spirit into Galilee, and a report concerning him went out through all the surrounding country. ¹⁵And he taught in their synagogues, being glorified by all. ¹⁶And he came to Nazareth, where he had been brought up; and he went to the synagogue, as his custom was, on the sabbath day. And he stood up to read; ¹⁷and there was given to him the book of the prophet Isaiah. He opened the book and found the place where it was written,

¹⁸"The Spirit of the Lord is upon me,
because he has anointed me to preach
good news to the poor.
He has sent me to proclaim release to
the captives
and recovering of sight to the blind,
to set at liberty those who are oppressed,
¹⁹to proclaim the acceptable year of the
Lord."

²⁰And he closed the book, and gave it back to the attendant, and sat down; and the eyes of all in the synagogue were fixed on him. ²¹And he began to say to them, "Today this scripture has been fulfilled in your hearing." ²²And all spoke well of him, and wondered at the gracious words which proceeded out of his mouth; and they said, "Is not this Joseph's son?" ²³And he said to them, "Doubtless you will quote to me this proverb, 'Physician, heal yourself; what we have heard you did at Capernaum, do here also in your own country.'" ²⁴And he said, "Truly, I say to you, no prophet is acceptable in his own country. ²⁵But in truth, I tell you, there were many widows in Israel in the days of Elijah, when the heaven was shut up three years and six months, when there came a great famine over all the land; ²⁶and Elijah was sent to none of

> If you wish to receive the great Spirit of fire, so that he dwells in you, first offer physical labors and humility of heart and, lifting your thoughts to heaven day and night, seek this Spirit of fire with a righteous heart—and he will be given to you.
> —St. Anthony of Egypt

them but only to Zarephath, in the land of Sidon, to a woman who was a widow. [27]And there were many lepers in Israel in the time of the prophet Elisha; and none of them was cleansed, but only Naaman the Syrian." [28]When they heard this, all in the synagogue were filled with wrath. [29]And they rose up and put him out of the city, and led him to the brow of the hill on which their city was built, that they might throw him down headlong. [30]But passing through the midst of them he went away.

S ome thirty years have passed since our previous reading. Jesus has left Nazareth, his hometown, and has begun to teach in nearby towns. Now he returns to Nazareth to deliver an especially important homily.

Jesus' homily unfolds the meaning of a passage from the prophet Isaiah. Isaiah, with his declaration that "the Spirit of the Lord GOD is upon me" (61:1), spoke of some future person who was going to fulfill God's purposes—an agent of God who would release those in slavery, bring liberty to the oppressed, and give sight to the blind. Jesus' homily on this passage is short. "Today," he says, "this scripture has been fulfilled" (Luke 4:21). Jesus declares himself to be the agent of God's purposes whom Isaiah foretold.

What kind of release does Jesus bring? Quite simply, he brings release from *everything* that binds, enslaves, and oppresses human beings—from indebtedness and poverty, from political and economic oppression, from physical afflictions, from our sins, even from death.

Jesus begins to accomplish this liberation and healing even as the people of Nazareth sit and listen ("fulfilled in your hearing," Luke 4:21). Through his presence, he makes forgiveness and reconciliation with God available to his listeners. And his words have divine power: those who respond to his teaching will be transformed into men and women of peace, justice, and love—even of enemies. By the Spirit, they will work for liberation, justice, and healing, so that the world might become a place for the flourishing of human lives. Ultimately, Jesus will bring the present age to an end and inaugurate the age to come. Then, in God's kingdom in its fullness, he will give us total peace in God's presence forever.

Jesus affirms that the Spirit is empowering him to carry out this vast work. Here we meet a profound mystery: the relationship of Jesus and the Spirit. Jesus is the Son of God, and so the Spirit, who is the power and presence of God, is with him in an utterly unique way. Jesus once declared that he and the Father are one (see John 10:30). It is equally true that Jesus and the Spirit are one. To see Jesus at work is to witness the Spirit in action; to receive Jesus' teaching is to be nourished by the wisdom of the Spirit.

> **To see Jesus at work is to witness the Spirit in action.**

The people in Nazareth do not understand all of this. What they do understand, however, pleases them. They are politically and economically oppressed and are happy to hear that Jesus is bringing liberation. They have heard about his miraculous healings and welcome such healing power. Their question—"Is not this Joseph's son?" (Luke 4:22)—seems an expression not of incredulity but of approval. "How wonderful that our own Jesus, son of Joseph, is going to do this!"

Jesus had lived his whole life in Nazareth. So the Nazarenes look forward to Jesus using his newly revealed powers on their behalf. Perhaps they picture him as their town healer—a miracle-working magician providing healings for pay. There were such people in first-century Palestine (see Acts 8:9-24).

Jesus discerns their line of thought. He is saying, "I know you're going to quote the proverb 'Physician, heal yourself.'" The "self" the people have in mind is not Jesus (he is not sick) but themselves. As his family and townspeople, they regard themselves as part of him—a normal attitude in a family- and clan-based society. On this basis, they expect to be the main recipients of his healing gifts.

But Jesus has no intention of settling down in Nazareth again. He has left Nazareth for good in order to launch his mission. He foresees that as soon as he makes his intentions clear, his relatives and neighbors will swing around from approval to rejection. So he quotes this proverb: "No prophet is acceptable in his own country" (Luke 4:24).

Jesus communicates his intention for his ministry by referring to two Old Testament prophets, Elijah and Elisha. They didn't concentrate their God-given powers solely on fellow Israelites but worked life-giving miracles for pagans from Phoenicia and Syria. Similarly, Jesus implies, he has not come simply to care for "himself," that is, for his own relatives and neighbors and other fellow Jews. He has come to bring God's saving love to everyone (see Acts 1:8).

Sure enough, as soon as Jesus makes the breadth of his mission clear, his fellow townspeople turn against him. They are angered by the idea that God would not put them at the top of his list of beneficiaries. They see themselves as poor, captive, sick, and oppressed, and expect that if God is going to care for such people, *they* should be the first in line. "Forget all the poor, captive, blind, and oppressed Phoenicians, Syrians, and others! *We* are the people whom God favors!"

By his homily, Jesus in effect invites his townspeople to support his mission to the world. But they reject the invitation—and him.
For us, the incident carries important messages.

The action of the Spirit, which Jesus initiates, is one of release and restoration. The Spirit brings freedom to all who are enslaved. There is no sinful distortion of our true selves from which the Spirit will not free us and heal us.

Yet the thrust of the Spirit's action is not only toward us; it is toward the world. The Spirit does not come to fulfill *my* expectations for myself, *my* ideas of what my life should be. He gives me the opportunity to cooperate with *his* plans, *his* ideas of what I should be doing. This involves sharing in what the Spirit is doing for *others*. As long as I think that my life is mainly about me, the invitations of the Spirit will fall on my deaf ears—or even draw from me an angry rejection. Such self-centeredness is the primary oppression from which the Spirit comes to free us.

Understand!

1. What does it mean "to preach good news to the poor" (Luke 4:18)? To "proclaim the acceptable year of the Lord" (4:19)? How did Jesus do this?

_____

_____

_____

_____

_____

_____

2. Jesus went out of his way to confront the Nazarenes' misunderstanding of his ministry (Luke 4:23-27). Why was he willing to do so?

_____

_____

_____

_____

_____

_____

3. Luke describes how the people of Nazareth felt about Jesus when he preached to them. How do you think Jesus felt about them while he was preaching? When they were trying to kill him (see Luke 4:29)?

_____

_____

_____

_____

_____

_____

4. Presumably Mary was present during this incident. How do you think she felt about the day's events? How are these events connected to Simeon's words to her in the passage from our last session— Luke 2:35?

_____

_____

_____

_____

_____

_____

5. Why do you think the people refused to welcome the movement of the Spirit? What change was required of them? What might they have feared?

_____

_____

_____

_____

_____

_____

▶ In the Spotlight
The Synagogue

In his homily on Isaiah, Jesus sounded the keynote of his ministry to the world. Yet the audience he chose for his announcement was very small indeed. Luke says that Jesus preached in the synagogue in Nazareth. Even if every man, woman, and child in the village went to the synagogue that day, there would probably have been no more than four hundred people present—fewer than the number who attend Sunday Mass in many parishes today.

So far archaeologists have not found any first-century synagogues in Galilee. The earliest remains of ancient synagogues there date from the third century. The Greek word for synagogue means literally "gathering." So it could refer to an assembly of people as well as to a place of gathering. Some scholars speculate that in Jesus' time, Galilean Jews met in homes or outdoors. With a southern California-type climate, the weather in Galilee favors outdoor meetings much of the year. So Luke's statement that Jesus went into the synagogue might be taken to mean that he went to the gathering, wherever that was.

Homes in Nazareth were not spacious. If the residents of Nazareth held their sabbath gathering in a home, there could only have been a few dozen people present when Jesus declared his fulfillment of Isaiah's prophecy.

But perhaps the weather was fine and the villagers gathered outside in the shade of their olive trees. What an informal setting for one of the most important homilies ever preached!

Grow!

1. When have you experienced recovery of sight? Being set free? How have these experiences shaped your understanding of God?

_____

_____

_____

_____

_____

_____

2. Who are the poor in your world? Are some more visible than others? Do you know of someone who is poor because he or she is lonely or spiritually starved? What kinds of help do they need?

_____

_____

_____

_____

_____

_____

3. In specific, practical terms, how is Jesus calling you to participate in his mission to those who are poor or oppressed? In what way would this involve your working with others? In order to respond fully to Jesus' invitation, are there any expectations for your own life that you would need to set aside?

_____

_____

_____

_____

_____

_____

4. When have you realized that you were resisting the Spirit's action or guidance? What did you learn from this experience?

_____

_____

_____

_____

_____

_____

_____

5. Do your prayers tend to focus on your own needs? Why or why not? How could you cooperate with the Spirit's efforts to turn your attention to the needs of other people?

_____

_____

_____

_____

_____

_____

_____

▶ In the Spotlight
The Jubilee Year

Jesus declared that a prophecy of Isaiah applied to himself (see Luke 4:18-21). The passage in Isaiah that Jesus quoted contained an allusion to a yet earlier Scripture text. Isaiah's reference to an "acceptable year of the Lord" picked up the idea of a year of grace and favor in the Book of Leviticus.

Leviticus 25 speaks about a "jubilee" year, to be celebrated every fifty years, when people would remit debts and allow those who had fallen into servitude because of indebtedness to go free. Properties that had been seized for the nonpayment of debts would be restored to their original owners.

This law was designed for ancient Israel, which was a society composed mostly of small-scale farmers. In that society, social justice was based on every family having its own land. Inevitably, various factors disturbed this arrangement. Poorer farmers fell into debt. Eventually some lost their lands and were forced to become servants of others. To deal with these recurrent problems, the Mosaic law mandated the jubilee, which periodically restored freedom and land—and thus a measure of social justice.

By alluding to the jubilee, Isaiah communicates the message that God is going to restore justice to society. By picking up Isaiah's prophecy, Jesus proclaims that the restoration of justice has now begun.

Modern societies are structured differently from the peasant society of ancient Israel. Following Jesus in our more complex world today means finding new ways to implement the biblical ideal of social justice.

Reflect!

1. In what way are you poor, captive, blind, or oppressed? Do you look to the Holy Spirit to help you in your need? Reflect on this quietly. Then share your thoughts with God.

2. In the text from Isaiah that Jesus reads in the synagogue in Nazareth, "the acceptable year of the Lord" is an allusion to the following passage from Leviticus on the year of "jubilee." Reflect on this passage (see also the "In the Spotlight" section above):

> And you shall hallow the fiftieth year, and proclaim liberty throughout the land to all its inhabitants; it shall be a

jubilee for you, when each of you shall return to his prop-
erty and each of you shall return to his family. . . .

And if your brother becomes poor beside you, and sells
himself to you, you shall not make him serve as a slave; he
shall be with you as a hired servant and as a sojourner. He
shall serve with you until the year of the jubilee; then he
shall go out from you, he and his children with him, and
go back to his own family, and return to the possession
of his fathers. For they are my servants, whom I brought
forth out of the land of Egypt; they shall not be sold as
slaves. You shall not rule over him with harshness, but
shall fear your God.

—Leviticus 25:10, 39-43

3. Reflect on the continuation of the passage in Isaiah that
Jesus reads:

The Spirit of the Lord GOD is upon me,
    because the LORD has anointed me . . .
    to comfort all who mourn;
to grant to those who mourn in Zion—
    to give them a garland instead of ashes,
the oil of gladness instead of mourning,
    the mantle of praise instead of a faint spirit;
that they may be called oaks of righteousness,
    the planting of the LORD, that he may be glorified.
They shall build up the ancient ruins,
    they shall raise up the former devastations. . . .

—Isaiah 61:1, 2-4

▶ In the Spotlight
Through Praying for Another,
I Was Healed

Here is a testimony from a woman who experienced the liberation that Jesus promised:

An MRI showed a condition called spondyliothesis, caused by acute arthritis that had worn out the facet joints in my vertebrae. The back specialist recommended some spinal epidural injections, which did nothing. The next step was surgery. In the meantime the pain was making me miserable and short-tempered with my family. . . . I spent hours just hanging over an exercise ball, in tears, trying to relieve the pain, and I was taking the dose of painkiller used to treat cancer patients.

Then it happened, quietly, quickly, and unexpectedly. I went to my prayer meeting early and was praying before the Blessed Sacrament. My hands felt as if they were being anointed, and the Lord prompted me to go and pray for one of the other members of the prayer group. This person had heart problems and was scheduled for surgery in the next couple of days.

I laid my hands on this man and prayed in tongues. I could feel the power of the Spirit moving through my hands to him, and he said to me, "Now I know I will be OK."

Then he started to pray for me, and I could feel the power of the Spirit coming through his hands. It was like a little whirlwind, with the Holy Spirit moving between the two of us, going out from me to him and also from him to me. . . .

When I went home that night, I was tired and forgot to take my painkillers. When I awoke in the morning, the pain was completely gone.

—**Anne from Canada,** taken from *When the Spirit Speaks*

Act!

Look back at Questions 2 and 3 in the "Grow!" section on page 55. In light of your reflections on these questions, decide to take one practical step to come to the aid of someone in need. Ask the Holy Spirit to guide you.

▶ In the Spotlight
Today!

After reading the text from Isaiah, Jesus rolled up the scroll, looked at his listeners, and declared, "Today this scripture has been fulfilled in your hearing" (Luke 4:21). One can almost feel the electricity of that *today!* At that very moment, God was fulfilling the promises awaited for so many centuries.

We might feel a bit of nostalgia for that day back then in Nazareth. If only we had been there to hear Jesus speak those words. If only we could have been with him when he said, "Today!"

There's no need for nostalgia. We haven't missed anything by living in the twenty-first rather than the first century, because the Holy Spirit is with us. The Spirit brings the full reality of Jesus to us here and now.

Jesus later told his disciples not to be sad that he was leaving them, because it was to their advantage—his departure would open the way for the coming of the Spirit (see John 16:7). Now that the Spirit has come, he makes Jesus and his teaching and healing present to us today.

This is true in a special way in the celebration of the Eucharist. In the Eucharist, Jesus' earthly ministry, his Last Supper, his death, and his resurrection become present to us by the power of the Holy Spirit.

Here, There, and Everywhere

Acts 8:26-40

26But an angel of the Lord said to Philip, "Rise and go toward the south to the road that goes down from Jerusalem to Gaza." This is a desert road. 27And he rose and went. And behold, an Ethiopian, a eunuch, a minister of the Candace, queen of the Ethiopians, in charge of all her treasure, had come to Jerusalem to worship 28and was returning; seated in his chariot, he was reading the prophet Isaiah. 29And the Spirit said to Philip, "Go up and join this chariot." 30So Philip ran to him, and heard him reading Isaiah the prophet, and asked, "Do you understand what you are reading?" 31And he said, "How can I, unless some one guides me?" And he invited Philip to come up and sit with him. 32 Now the passage of the scripture which he was reading was this:

> Resolve to accept willingly all the inspirations it may please God to send you.
> —St. Francis de Sales, *Introduction to the Devout Life*

"As a sheep led to the slaughter
or a lamb before its shearer is dumb,
so he opens not his mouth.
33In his humiliation justice was denied him.
Who can describe his generation?
For his life is taken up from the earth."

34And the eunuch said to Philip, "About whom, pray, does the prophet say this, about himself or about some one else?" 35Then Philip opened his mouth, and beginning with this scripture he told him the good news of Jesus. 36And as they went along the road they came to some water, and the eunuch said, "See, here is water! What is to prevent my being baptized?" 38And he commanded the chariot to stop, and they both went down into the water, Philip and the eunuch, and he baptized him. 39And when they came up out of the water, the Spirit of the Lord caught up Philip; and the eunuch saw him no more, and went on his way rejoicing. 40But Philip was found at Azotus, and passing on he preached the gospel to all the towns till he came to Caesarea.

Taa he time: not long after the coming of the Spirit to the disciples on Pentecost. The place: not far from Jerusalem. The characters: a leader among the Jerusalem Christians named Philip, and an Ethiopian government official, unnamed.

Philip has been evangelizing in the countryside with the apostles Peter and John. The Ethiopian has been worshiping in the Temple in Jerusalem—apparently he is a devout, non-Jewish believer in the God of Israel—and now he is on his way home. Luke calls him a "eunuch," but he is not necessarily emasculated, since the term may simply accompany his official title.

In the usual course of events, the two men would probably never meet. But the Spirit is not limited by the usual course of events.

As the scene opens, the Ethiopian is riding along in a fancy carriage. His vehicle marks him as a wealthy man, as does his owning a biblical scroll. The passage he is reading speaks about a servant of God who "has borne our griefs and carried our sorrows." Isaiah says that "he was wounded for our transgressions . . . ; / upon him was the chastisement that made us whole, / and with his stripes we are healed." The healing concerns the forgiveness of sins, for the servant "bore the sin of many, / and made intercession for the transgressors" (Isaiah 53:4-5, 12).

Not surprisingly, the Ethiopian is puzzled by this obscure prophecy. But his puzzlement creates a teachable moment, and the Spirit sends just the person to help him. "Run after the carriage and talk to that man," the Spirit says to Philip (see Acts 8:29).

Philip sprints after the carriage—given ancient road conditions, it probably isn't moving very fast—and runs alongside. Apparently the Ethiopian doesn't notice Philip bobbing along next to his carriage and goes on with his reading. As was customary at that time, he reads aloud, even when he is by himself.

At this point, Philip has run out of guidance from the Spirit. But, using an obvious conversation starter, he asks the Ethiopian if he understands what he is reading. "Not really," the Ethiopian replies. Philip's question implies that he knows something about the Bible, so the Ethiopian invites him into his limousine (see Acts 8:30-31).

Philip explains that the text speaks about Jesus. From an explanation of Isaiah, Philip moves on to an account of Jesus' life and ministry. Undoubtedly at the heart of Philip's account is Jesus' death and resurrection—and the gift of the Spirit.

As Philip talks, the significance of the gospel breaks into the Ethiopian's mind and heart. He realizes that Jesus gave his life for *him*.

The road from Jerusalem to Gaza goes through dry country, but there are some springs along the way. Perhaps pointing to such a spring, the Ethiopian asks Philip why he shouldn't be baptized right away. Philip sees no objection.

> The Spirit was crossing ethnic and cultural boundaries to make Jesus known, and Philip was going along.

Immediately after the baptism, the Spirit separates the two men. Philip is transported to a nearby city—the most dramatic movement by the Spirit of any we read about in this book! The Ethiopian resumes his journey, but he is changed. He goes on his way rejoicing (see Acts 8:36-39).

Philip and the Ethiopian were together only long enough for a single conversation. Even if it were a long conversation, it was a short program of initiation. Compare it to today's year long Rite of Christian Initiation for Adults! Yet Philip has communicated the core of the gospel, and the Ethiopian has decided to follow Jesus.

It is instructive to total up what the Spirit does in this episode. He guides Philip to speak with a stranger—capitalizing on a rich opportunity. He provides the Ethiopian official with an inspired interpretation of Scripture, showing him that God has acted for him through Jesus. He gives the Ethiopian faith and a desire to be united to Jesus, and fills him with joy through baptism. Then he moves Philip on to other matters. The Spirit really works overtime here!

But, we might wonder, so what? This is an unusual story. How likely is it that anything like this will happen to you or me?

Well, let's not be too quick to dismiss the possibility that the Spirit can guide us also in unexpected ways. The Spirit may not send you running across an airport. But he may spur you to strike up a conversation with the person in the next seat on the plane. Many a chance meeting by travelers has provided an opportunity for sharing the gospel.

Philip's conversation with the Ethiopian was uniquely orchestrated by the Spirit. Yet the Spirit gives all of us unique opportunities to serve him. Some may seem quite ordinary: a particular moment when you stand in a particular hospital room speaking to a particular friend, a particular moment when I am asked a question by a particular high school student in a religious education class. No one but you or me will be there to serve the Spirit's purposes. Moments like these are *our* unique opportunities to sense the Spirit's presence and receive his guidance in order to make Jesus known. Will we be as ready to respond as Philip was?

It is worth observing that Philip wasn't sharing mere personal opinions when he explained the passage from Isaiah to the Ethiopian. Philip had been working with the apostles Peter and John (see Acts 8:4-25). The apostles gained insights into how the Isaiah passage speaks about Jesus, and Philip undoubtedly learned from them. So

Philip was taught before he taught others. In him, we see that religious education isn't the opposite of being led by the Spirit. The two go hand in hand.

Before the present incident, Philip was busy evangelizing Samaritans. In our reading, he spends time with an Ethiopian. Afterward, he goes on to Caesarea, a city where most of the people he will meet are gentiles. We don't know whether, before he became a Christian, Philip associated with or even liked Samaritans, Ethiopians, and other non-Jews. But the Spirit was crossing ethnic and cultural boundaries to make Jesus known, and Philip was going along.

The Spirit is doing the same today. Are you going with him?

Understand!

1. Put yourself in Philip's place. How would you explain the passage in Isaiah (Acts 8:32-33) to someone who asked you? How would you briefly explain who Jesus is, what he has done, and what it means for us? What other Scripture passages might you use?

_____

_____

_____

_____

_____

_____

2. The Ethiopian responds quickly to Philip's presentation of the gospel. After just a single conversation, he is ready to be baptized. Have you ever had a conversation in which something about God's relationship with you suddenly became clearer? Why, on the other hand, does understanding the gospel also take a long time?

_____

_____

_____

_____

_____

_____

_____

3. To Philip's question, "Do you understand what you are reading?" the Ethiopian answers, "How can I, unless some one guides me?" (Acts 8:30-31). What kinds of help do we need in order to truly understand the Bible? What kinds of help does the Church offer us? Which have you taken advantage of?

_____

_____

_____

_____

_____

_____

_____

4. In this episode, Philip was instantly available to the Spirit. How would you describe Philip's relationship with the Holy Spirit? How can a person grow in being attuned and open to the Spirit?

_____

_____

_____

_____

_____

_____

5. From what Luke tells us about the Ethiopian in this incident, what kind of man does he seem to have been?

_____

_____

_____

_____

_____

▶ In the Spotlight
Evangelization by Way of Disaster

The government official baptized by Philip returned home to Ethiopia. And then what? Did he spread the gospel? Did other Ethiopians become Christians? Perhaps a few did. But the large-scale evangelization of Ethiopia did not occur until three centuries later. And it happened by accident.

The accident involved a man named Frumentius, from the city of Tyre (in modern Lebanon), some time near the beginning of the fourth century. The account that survives is sketchy. But it seems that Frumentius took a trip through the Red Sea. Unfortunately, his ship sank near the African coast. At the time, this must have seemed like an unmitigated disaster. But it turned out to be a fortunate event for Ethiopia. (Is there such a thing as being shipwrecked in the Spirit? See Acts 27.)

Frumentius got to shore and traveled inland to Aksum, the capital of Ethiopia at that time. There he met the emperor and his son. Frumentius was a Christian, and he shared the gospel with the two royal figures. The son, Ezana, became a believer. In 330, when Ezana succeeded to the throne, he established Christianity as the religion of the land.

At this point, Frumentius traveled north to Egypt to consult with the bishop of Alexandra, the great Athanasius. St. Athanasius ordained Frumentius a bishop and sent him back to spearhead the continuing evangelization of Ethiopia.

Christianity took deep root in Ethiopia. Historically, the church in Ethiopia has had strong ties with the church in Egypt. At present, about two-thirds of Ethiopians are Christians. The great majority belong to the Ethiopian Orthodox Church. There is also a small Catholic minority.

Grow!

1. First an angel, then the Spirit guides Philip (see Acts 8:26, 29). God guides us in various ways. How have you experienced God's guidance? What have you learned about identifying—and authenticating—what seems to be guidance from the Holy Spirit?

_____

_____

_____

_____

_____

_____

_____

2. How often do you have the opportunity to witness to your faith? What parts of your own experience could you bring in to help others understand the meaning of the gospel for their own life? What effect do you think sharing your testimony in this way might have on family members who are not close to the Lord?

_____

_____

_____

_____

_____

_____

_____

3. A passage in Isaiah had a big impact on the Ethiopian. When has a specific Scripture passage made a big impact on you?

_____

_____

_____

_____

_____

_____

4. Philip was a leader in the church in Jerusalem (see Acts 6:1-6). Are official leaders of the Church the only ones responsible for making Jesus known in the world? What is _your_ share in this task? What practical steps could you take so that you exercise this responsibility more often? How can the Holy Spirit guide you?

_____

_____

_____

_____

_____

5. How could you support your parish's program for preparing people for baptism or reception into the Church? Is there anyone you might invite to participate? Are there other evangelization or religious education programs you could participate in?

_____

_____

_____

_____

_____

_____

_____

▶ In the Spotlight
Accept All Charisms!

Charisms are graces given by the Holy Spirit that empower us to carry on Christ's work in the world. In Romans 12:6-8, St. Paul mentions some of these gifts, including prophecy, service, teaching, exhortation, almsgiving, aiding others, and acts of mercy. In 1 Corinthians 12:8-10, Paul lists such charisms as speaking with wisdom, exercising faith, working miracles, discerning spirits, speaking in tongues, and interpreting speech in tongues. The Catholic Church says this about charisms:

Charisms are to be accepted with gratitude by the person who receives them and by all members of the Church as well. They are a wonderfully rich grace for the apostolic vitality and for the holiness of the entire Body of Christ, provided they really are genuine gifts of the Holy Spirit and are used in full conformity with authentic promptings of this same Spirit, that is, in keeping with charity, the true measure of all charisms. (*Catechism of the Catholic Church*, 800)

Reflect!

1. The Spirit's forceful interventions in Philip's life show that sometimes the Spirit wishes to break through our routines and lead us to serve him in new ways. The incident suggests that when we cooperate, the Spirit will accomplish great things in the lives of others. Spend some time reflecting on whether you are willing to say yes to the Holy Spirit in whatever ways he might wish to guide and use you in advancing Christ's kingdom. Express your thoughts to God.

2. Read and reflect on the passage in Isaiah that Philip and the Ethiopian discussed. What is God saying to you in this passage? Is there something here for you to share with someone else?

> Who has believed what we have heard?
>> And to whom has the arm of the LORD been revealed?
> For he grew up before him like a young plant,
>> and like a root out of dry ground;
> he had no form or comeliness that we should look at him,
>> and no beauty that we should desire him.
> He was despised and rejected by men;
>> a man of sorrows, and acquainted with grief;
> and as one from whom men hide their faces
>> he was despised, and we esteemed him not.
>
> Surely he has borne our griefs
>> and carried our sorrows;
> yet we esteemed him stricken,
>> smitten by God, and afflicted.
> But he was wounded for our transgressions,
>> he was bruised for our iniquities;
> upon him was the chastisement that made us whole,

and with his stripes we are healed.
All we like sheep have gone astray;
    we have turned every one to his own way;
and the LORD has laid on him
    the iniquity of us all.

He was oppressed, and he was afflicted,
    yet he opened not his mouth;
like a lamb that is led to the slaughter,
    and like a sheep that before its shearers is dumb,
    so he opened not his mouth.
        . . . He was cut off out of the land of the living,
        stricken for the transgression of my people?
And they made his grave with the wicked
    and with a rich man in his death,
although he had done no violence,
    and there was no deceit in his mouth.

Yet it was the will of the LORD to bruise him;
    he has put him to grief;
when he makes himself an offering for sin,
    he shall see his offspring, he shall prolong his days;
the will of the LORD shall prosper in his hand; . . .
by his knowledge shall the righteous one, my servant,
    make many to be accounted righteous;
    and he shall bear their iniquities.
. . . He poured out his soul to death,
    and was numbered with the transgressors;
yet he bore the sin of many,
    and made intercession for the transgressors.

—Isaiah 53:1-12

▶ In the Spotlight
Trust God and Work Hard!

Frances Xavier Cabrini (1850–1917), an Italian who became a U.S. citizen, was the first American to be canonized. She wrote this to encourage her sisters in the Missionary Sisters of the Sacred Heart, the order which she founded:

How pleasing it is to the Holy Ghost to see zealous souls that seek to spread the Kingdom of Jesus Christ! We give divine homage when we convert a sinner, or make known more clearly and more distinctly the knowledge of Jesus Christ. Work, work indefatigably, without tiring, for the salvation of souls. May the Holy Spirit work in you, pray with you, and communicate to you his lights, graces, and treasures. If you are zealous, he will really enlighten you with his divine Light. He will assist you in your work and trials. He will support you in danger, defend you from internal and external enemies, and strengthen you by his virtue. Have faith, great faith, faith and confidence, and pray constantly. The Holy Spirit, with his immense charity, will then diffuse himself in your hearts and in your souls in order to make them stronger with his own fortitude.

—**St. Frances Cabrini,** *The Travels of Mother Frances Xavier Cabrini*

Act!

Decide that if during the next twenty-four hours, you think the Holy Spirit is guiding you to do something, you will do it. As preparation for discerning whether what you feel prompted to do really comes from the Spirit, take a few minutes to read St. Paul's words about love in 1 Corinthians 13:4-7 and his words about the fruit of the Spirit in Galatians 5:22-23 (and see the counsel of Columba Marmion below).

▶ In the Spotlight
Discernment

Columba Marmion (1858–1923) was a Belgian monk recognized for his gift of spiritual counsel. In a letter to a friend, he explained how a person can distinguish the promptings of the Holy Spirit from those of other spirits. Concerning evils spirits, he wrote:

You will always know them by their fruits, even though Satan may try to clothe himself as an angel of light. Our Lord says: "You will know them by their fruits" (Matthew 7:16). You will recognize these spirits by the fruits they produce in your soul. God's Spirit, even when he reproaches us, or inclines us to confusion, or compunction for our sins, *ever* fills the soul with peace, and filial confidence in our heavenly Father. The other spirits dry up our souls . . . or . . . casts gloom and discouragement into our soul.

—**Columba Marmion**, *The English Letters of Columba Marmion*

Kindness and Charity

Acts 9:31-43

³¹The church throughout all Judea and Galilee and Samaria had peace and was built up; and walking in the fear of the Lord and in the comfort of the Holy Spirit it was multiplied.

³²Now as Peter went here and there among them all, he came down also to the saints that lived at Lydda. ³³There he found a man names Aeneas, who had been bedridden for eight years and was paralyzed. ³⁴And Peter said to him, "Aeneas, Jesus Christ heals you; rise and make your bed." And immediately he rose. ³⁵And all the residents of Lydda and Sharon saw him, and they turned to the Lord.

³⁶Now there was at Joppa a disciple named Tabitha, which means Dorcas or Gazelle. She was full of good works and acts of charity. ³⁷In those days she fell sick and died; and when they had washed her, they laid her in an upper room. ³⁸Since Lydda was near Joppa, the disciples, hearing that Peter was there, sent two men to him entreating him, "Please come to us without delay." ³⁹So Peter rose and went with them. And when he had come, they took him to the upper room. All the widows stood beside him weeping, and showing tunics and other garments which Dorcas made while she was with them. ⁴⁰But Peter put them all outside and knelt down and prayed; then turning to the body he said, "Tabitha, rise." And she opened her eyes, and when she saw Peter she sat up. ⁴¹And he gave her his hand and lifted her up. Then calling the saints and widows he presented her alive. ⁴²And it became known throughout all Joppa, and many believed in the Lord. ⁴³And he stayed in Joppa for many days with one Simon, a tanner.

> Whether extraordinary or simple and humble, charisms are graces of the Holy Spirit which directly or indirectly benefit the Church, ordered as they are to her building up, to the good of men, and to the needs of the world.
> —*Catechism of the Catholic Church*, 799

Y ou might expect that the two miracles worked by the Holy Spirit through Peter—the healing of Aeneas and the restoration of Tabitha's life—would be the focus of our session. But instead, I want to focus on the Spirit's action in Tabitha before she got sick and died.

It is good to meditate on the Spirit's working in astounding ways, like healing paralysis and restoring a dead person to life. On most days of the week, however, we may get more benefit from meditating on the Spirit's less conspicuous ways of acting in our lives. I'm not denying that even today, the Spirit sometimes does the kinds of things we see him doing through Peter in this reading. But the Spirit is *constantly* involved in the type of work we hear about Tabitha doing—caring for people in need.

In fact, the different kinds of spiritual activity we see in Peter and Tabitha are not in conflict. They go together. Discussing spiritual gifts, St. Paul says the Spirit gives the Church both "healers" and "helpers" (1 Corinthians 12:28).

Luke writes that "the church . . . was built up" and was "walking in the fear of the Lord and in the comfort of the Holy Spirit" (Acts 9:31). The two episodes in our reading show us what this looked like on the ground. We see Peter, traveling from community to community, working miracles of healing in the power of the Spirit. And we get a complementary picture of Tabitha, who stays home and alleviates the distress of her impoverished neighbors. Her activities are not miraculous, but they are just as much works of the Spirit as the healings performed by Peter. Through her, people experience the "comfort of the Holy Spirit."

Tabitha is "full of good works and acts of charity" (Acts 9:36). Apparently, she has material resources at her disposal: She can afford to buy fabric and has free time for making it into clothing.

And she owns a two-story house (Acts 9:37). What she has, she uses for others.

Luke calls Tabitha a "disciple." Thus, he rates her alongside Jesus' more prominent disciples, such as Peter, John, and James. This is high praise. But she is not the kind of disciple who had followed Jesus along the roads of Palestine or now travels from place to place evangelizing. Tabitha is a stay-at-home disciple.

When did Tabitha become a follower of Jesus? We simply don't know. Did she, like Peter and Philip, experience sudden, unexpected leadings of the Spirit? We don't know that either. We do know that the Spirit could be seen in her life. Through Tabitha, as much as through Peter and Philip, the Church was being "built up" and was "walking in the fear of the Lord" and "multiplied" (Acts 9:31).

> The Spirit may direct our attention no farther than to the family across the street.

In Peter, with great drama, and in Tabitha, with quieter acts of charity, we see the fulfillment of Jesus' words in the synagogue in Nazareth: "The Spirit of the Lord is upon me . . . to preach good news to the poor. He has sent me to proclaim release to the captives" (Luke 4:18).

In that synagogue sermon, Jesus indicated the outward thrust of his mission into the world (see Luke 4:14-30). And we saw a dramatic example of this outward movement of the Spirit in our last session in the story about Philip (see Acts 8:26-40). With Tabitha, we see that moving outward with the Spirit does not necessarily mean leaving the country, or even leaving town. The Spirit may direct our attention no farther than to the family across the street—or in the next apartment.

The contrast of Tabitha and Philip is striking. His encounter with the Ethiopian official is extraordinary to the point of seeming bizarre. The Spirit's action in Tabitha is so hidden in the ordinary that we are in danger of not noticing it at all.

In any case, when Tabitha dies, the Christian community sends word to Peter to come right away (see Acts 9:38). On his arrival, Peter finds the women grieving. Luke says that the grief-stricken widows were "showing" the clothing Tabitha had made for them. The Greek text can be taken to mean that they were actually wearing these clothes as they showed them to Peter.

Peter prays, then speaks directly and simply to Tabitha: "Rise" (Acts 9:40). The Spirit does not require a lengthy discourse or magical mumbo jumbo. In this Spirit-filled command, Peter sounds like his Master in an earlier episode (see Mark 5:41).

What joy Tabitha's community must have felt at her restoration! Her presence with them again was a powerful sign of Jesus' resurrection and the gift of the Spirit—and a delight for all who loved her. I suspect that after the hoopla died down, she celebrated by taking up her sewing again.

To Tabitha, now among the recognized saints with the Lord (see page 91), we might address a prayer or two:

"St. Tabitha, raised to life by the power of the Spirit: that we might respond to the Spirit's call to rise to new life, pray for us!"

"St. Tabitha, devoted to the care of your neighbors in need: that we might open our eyes and hearts to those whom the Spirit urges us to help, pray for us!"

Understand!

1. Luke tells us that Tabitha was "full of good works" (Acts 9:36). What does this suggest about the kind of person she was and how she lived her life? What do you think motivated her?

_____

_____

_____

_____

_____

_____

_____

2. When Tabitha died, the Christian community sent word to Peter to come "without delay" (Acts 9:38). Why did they want him to come immediately? Were they expecting a miracle?

_____

_____

_____

_____

_____

_____

3. The poor women whom Tabitha helped were grief stricken at her death (see Acts 9:39). In what ways do you think they would miss her?

_____

_____

_____

_____

_____

4. What reason might Peter have had for sending everyone out of the room (see Acts 9:40)?

_____

_____

_____

_____

_____

_____

5. Peter does not mention Jesus in his command to Tabitha (see Acts 9:40). How does Luke indicate that the power that restored Tabitha's life came from Jesus rather than Peter?

_____

_____

_____

_____

_____

_____

▶ In the Spotlight
Listening to the Spirit

Here's an example of how the Spirit guides us to help one another:

When our family lived in Minneapolis, I saw in a store one day a beautiful, one-hundred-percent wool sweater, size medium, for $6.40. I immediately thought of John R., a good friend who had lived with us for two years and had worked at one time with my husband. John didn't have a lot of money because he had taken a job that allowed him time to work with the Hmong, the mountain people of Vietnam [Laos], many of whom relocated to Minneapolis after the [Vietnam] war.

I bought the sweater for John and wrapped it up, although it wasn't his birthday. I had never given him a gift before, nor have I since. Bill, a neighbor who worked with John, stopped by that evening and took the present to give to John the next day.

John stopped by the next day to tell me the beautiful way God had blessed him. Earlier that week he had been with a Hmong friend at his apartment. It was very cold, and he decided to give his friend his favorite sweater, which was heavy and warm. The very next day he went to work and received a new wool sweater!

Praise God for his faithfulness to his children! For me this was a confirmation that God is speaking to me and that I am able to hear and respond to him.

—**Deanna from Michigan,** from *When the Spirit Speaks*

Grow!

1. Think of one or two people you know who are like Tabitha. How do they decide which of the many needs around them to address? How do they organize their time? What role do you think the Holy Spirit plays in their decisions of whom to help and where to spend their time?

2. Recall a time when you were prompted by the Holy Spirit to help someone in some way. How did the Spirit lead you? What was the outcome? How can you be more open to the Spirit's promptings in this regard?

_____

_____

_____

_____

_____

_____

3. How are you making your material resources available to help others? What obstacles may be preventing you from being more generous with either your time or your resources? How might you overcome these obstacles?

_____

_____

_____

_____

_____

_____

4. In what ways do the Spirit's spectacular workings and his less obvious workings both contribute to the Church's life and mission? When have you seen either or both in action?

_____

_____

_____

_____

_____

_____

5. In what ways does Peter's behavior in these two incidents set an example for all of us? How could you exercise your faith in a bolder way? What might be keeping you from doing so?

_____

_____

_____

_____

_____

_____

▶ In the Spotlight
Do Good, Don't Fantasize

Francis de Sales helps us to recognize all the little opportunities that come our way to serve God.

There are people who imagine doing great things for God, things that would involve great suffering and heroic actions. Yet there is no opportunity to perform such deeds—and perhaps there never will be. They believe that just by imagining these deeds, they have shown great love, but they are often deceived. For while they desire to embrace great future crosses, they anxiously avoid the much lighter burdens that are presented to them now. Isn't it a big temptation to be heroic in imagination, but cowardly in carrying it out!

God, preserve us from these imaginary fervors, which so often produce a vain and secret pride in the bottom of our hearts! Great works do not always come our way, but in every moment, we may do little ones well—that is, with great love. Look at that saint, I ask you, who gives a cup of cold water to a thirsty traveler. He does only a small deed outwardly, but the intention, the kindness, the love which inspires him is so wonderful that it turns this simple cup of water into the water of life, and of eternal life.

The bees gather honey from the lily, the iris, and the rose, yet they get as much honey from the minute rosemary flowers and thyme. In fact, they draw not only more honey, but even better honey from these, for in small vessels the honey is more concentrated and better preserved. It is true: in the little works of devotion, love is not only practiced more frequently but usually more humbly as well, and consequently more usefully and productively.

—St. Francis de Sales, *Treatise on the Love of God*

Reflect!

1. Reflect on the following passage in which St. Paul instructs us on the gifts of the Spirit. What gifts is the Spirit giving you? Are you using them? Are you using them in love?

> And God has appointed . . . first apostles, second prophets, third teachers, then workers of miracles, then healers, helpers, administrators, speakers in various kinds of tongues. Are all apostles? Are all prophets? Are all teachers? Do all work miracles? Do all possess gifts of healing? Do all speak with tongues? . . . But earnestly desire the higher gifts.
>
> And I will show you a still more excellent way.
>
> If I speak in the tongues of men and of angels, but have not love, I am a noisy gong or a clanging cymbal. And if I have prophetic powers, and understand all mysteries

and all knowledge, and if I have all faith, so as to remove mountains, but have not love, I am nothing. If I give away all I have, and if I deliver my body to be burned, but have not love, I gain nothing.

—1 Corinthians 12:28–13:3

2. Read and reflect on two other passages in Acts that speak about the variety of ways the Spirit was at work in the early Christians:

Fear came upon every soul; and many wonders and signs were done through the apostles. And all who believed were together and had all things in common; and they sold their possessions and goods and distributed them to all, as any had need. And day by day, attending the temple together and breaking bread in their homes, they partook of food with glad and generous hearts, praising God and having favor with all the people. And the Lord added to their number day by day those who were being saved.

—Acts 2:43-47

Now the company of those who believed were of one heart and soul, and no one said that any of the things which he possessed was his own, but they had everything in common. And with great power the apostles gave their testimony to the resurrection of the Lord Jesus, and great grace was upon them all. There was not a needy person among them, for as many as were possessors of lands or houses sold them, and brought the proceeds of what was sold and laid it at the apostles' feet; and distribution was made to each as any had need.

—Acts 4:32-35

▶ In the Spotlight
"I Can Ask God for Anything"

In our reading, St. Peter sets an example of faith in the Holy Spirit's desire to heal. One way we can imitate Peter is suggested by high school teacher David Mangan.

Not long ago I was sharing with a group of high school students. They took me at my word about God's wanting to bless us and asked if we could pray for some of them who wanted to be healed. I didn't feel particularly faith-filled, but I figured I needed to act on what I had said.

We prayed for one girl with a chronic stomachache, and her pain went away immediately. Another student wanted prayer for a painful wrist. Again, after we prayed the pain left immediately. A third student had injured her ankle and was supposed to get a cast put on the following day. When we prayed the pain left, and the following day her doctors said that a cast was no longer necessary. I don't think our faith was perfect; we were just willing to act.

Prayer for healing may sound intimidating. My first thought when someone asks me to pray for healing is that I can't heal anyone—and that's absolutely true. However, I can pray, and my approach is simple.

I can always ask God for anything. I figure that he is interested in whatever the matter is because he is interested in me. I can't guarantee the results, but I can always do my part, and I can be sure that God will do his part. My part is to pray, and God's part is to love us however he chooses.

Amazingly, God often does heal the person I am praying for. When the prayer isn't answered in the way I want, then I have

to trust. I can't do God's job, but I can do mine. I can pray and
trust and I can encourage others to do the same.
—**David Mangan**, *God Loves You and There's Nothing You
Can Do About It*

Act!

Resolve to do something for someone this week in the spirit of
Tabitha. Remember: it's better to decide on something small and do
it than decide on something big and not do it.

▶ In the Spotlight
Calendar Connections

Some of the people and events we have been reading about are
regularly celebrated in the liturgy. St. Tabitha, for example, has
a feast day on the calendars of the Church in both the West
and the East: October 25. St. Philip, the star of our reading in
the last session, has two feast days: in the West, June 6; in the
Byzantine tradition, January 4.

The events in our first two readings also have feast days. The
episode in our first reading, the Visitation, is celebrated on May
31 in the West and on March 30 in the East. The Presentation
(our second reading), or as it is called in the Byzantine tradition, the Meeting with Our Lord and Savior Jesus Christ, is celebrated on February 2 in both the West and the East.

These feasts provide opportunities to reread the Scripture
passages and consider anew the Spirit's action in our lives. Here
are some further ways to celebrate the feasts: go to Mass, light
a candle and read the passage aloud, read a biography of the

saint, write a prayer asking the saint's intercession, or ask the saint to intercede for someone else you know.

By the way, Jesus' homily in Nazareth (our reading in Session 3) is read in the Roman liturgy on the Third and Fourth Sundays in Ordinary Time, Year C. Our final reading, in the next session, from 2 Corinthians 3–5, is read on the Ninth and Tenth Sundays in Ordinary Time, Year B.

Becoming What We See

2 Corinthians 3:17–5:5

3:17Now the Lord is the Spirit, and where the Spirit of the Lord is, there is freedom. 18And we all, with unveiled face, beholding the glory of the Lord, are being changed into his likeness from one degree of glory to another; for this comes from the Lord who is the Spirit.

> The Holy Spirit . . . is the identical Spirit which inspired Jesus in every act and thought; and it is by union with him that the interior of Jesus Christ is formed in our hearts.
> —Blessed Columba Marmion

4:1Therefore . . . we do not lose heart. . . . 6For it is the God who said, "Let light shine out of darkness," who has shone in our hearts to give the light of the knowledge of the glory of God in the face of Christ.

7But we have this treasure in earthen vessels, to show that the transcendent power belongs to God and not to us. 8We are afflicted in every way, but not crushed; perplexed, but not driven to despair; 9persecuted, but not forsaken; struck down, but not destroyed; 10always carrying in the body the death of Jesus, so that the life of Jesus may also be manifested in our bodies. 11For while we live we are always being given up to death for Jesus' sake, so that the life of Jesus may be manifested in our mortal flesh. 12So death is at work in us, but life in you. . . .

16So we do not lose heart. Though our outer nature is wasting away, our inner nature is being renewed every day. 17For this slight momentary affliction is preparing for us an eternal weight of glory beyond all comparison, 18because we look not to the things that are seen but to the things that are unseen; for the things that are seen are transient, but the things that are unseen are eternal.

5:1For we know that if the earthly tent we live in is destroyed, we have a building from God, a house not made with hands, eternal in the heavens. 2Here indeed we groan, and long to put on our heavenly dwelling, 3so that by putting it on we may not be found naked. ⁴For while we are still in this tent, we sigh with anxiety; not that we would be unclothed, but that we would be further clothed, so that what is mortal may be swallowed up by life. ⁵He who has prepared us for this very thing is God, who has given us the Spirit as a guarantee.

We see Jesus, Paul declares (see 2 Corinthians 3:18), not with our eyes, but with our hearts. This is no mere exercise of imagination, for Jesus' presence with us is more real than the material world our eyes do see. By the Spirit living in us, Jesus is directly present to us. There is no barrier, no veil, between us (see 4:6).

Looking at Jesus, we see God, for Jesus is the Son of God, "the likeness of God" (2 Corinthians 4:4). Looking at Jesus, we also see our own humanity, for he is the perfect human being. In him, we see what it is to be a complete human being and live a truly human life. Jesus shows us that our true humanity lies in being motivated by love for God and love for other people.

And as we look at Jesus, the Spirit transforms us into a likeness of what we see. Through our praying and celebrating the liturgy, studying and pondering Jesus' life, and putting his teaching into practice, the Spirit recreates us in his image.

This process is, fundamentally, the work of the Spirit. But ours is not a passive, sit-back-and-let-it-happen role. Look at Paul. He works night and day to carry out the service that God has entrusted to him (see 1 Corinthians 15:10). It is only because Paul is working so hard on his God-given assignment that he encounters so much suffering (see 2 Corinthians 4:8-12). Paul is a picture of active cooperation with the Spirit.

As we place ourselves at the disposal of the Spirit to be of service to other people, we run into obstacles of various kinds. These expose our flaws. We experience our weaknesses and vulnerabilities. But the Spirit will carry us through, Paul assures us. The Spirit enables us to imitate Jesus, who laid down his life for others (see Philippians 3:10). As we draw on the Spirit's power to imitate Jesus, the Spirit does indeed recreate us in his image. Thus, we become the persons that God has created us to be (see 2 Corinthians 4:16).

Paul rates his difficulties as great, but the Spirit as greater. Paul has often been at a loss, but never totally at a loss. He has been harassed by people, but never abandoned by God. As biblical scholar Ralph P. Martin puts it, Paul has been "knocked down, but not knocked out."

The tone of Paul's reflections on his sufferings is remarkably buoyant. We know that at times he felt heavily weighed down by his problems (see 2 Corinthians 1:8). But here he does not seem daunted by them. His listing of difficulties is shot through with a sense of the power of the Spirit at work in him (4:8-9). The more these difficulties uncover Paul's weaknesses, the more room the Spirit has to act in freedom in him and through him. By highlighting Paul's weaknesses, his difficulties highlight God's power.

Paul's experience reflects that of his Master. Jesus experienced human weakness in the extreme—being tortured to death. But in his weakness, the power of God was at work (see 1 Corinthians 1:22-25), overcoming death, removing sins, and bringing forth a new creation. It is this paradox of God's power at work in human weakness that Paul experiences.

Paul's efforts may not look glorious. Yet God's glory is present in the apostle's humble service. God's glory and Paul's self-giving love are one and the same. Thus, God's glory was nowhere more clearly manifested than on Golgotha, where Jesus accepted death for us (see John 12:27-33; 13:31-32; 17:1-5). So, too, God's glory is manifested in us when we share in Jesus' humble, loving service, despite the suffering that it entails. When we share his sufferings, Jesus is "manifested in our mortal flesh" (2 Corinthians 4:11). The power of the Spirit that makes it possible for us to participate in this process is the greatest "treasure" anyone can possess (see 4:7).

Our situation is deeply paradoxical. Our body, mind, and emotions are inevitably getting worn down through our afflictions, natural and man-made. Yet the very process of being worn down is essential for the Spirit's work of creating us anew (see 2 Corinthians 4:16-17). Because of the Spirit's presence in us, the forces that erode our earthly life open the door into God's glory. How the difficulties of this life can have such opposite effects on us is a deep mystery. It is the mystery that by dying we enter into life—the mystery of the cross.

> **God's glory is present in his humble service.**

Consequently, our prayer also is paradoxical. Paul speaks of our groaning, or sighing (see 2 Corinthians 5:1-5), as we express our sorrow to God, our discontent, our sadness at the condition of the world, our distress at our own weaknesses and failures and sins, our sufferings, physical and emotional. Yet our groaning is an expression of hope, because the Holy Spirit groans with us. The Spirit sighs in an appeal to God to fulfill his plans for us, to bring forth his new creation.

Because of the Spirit, the kingdom we long for is not entirely beyond the horizon in the far distant future. God has given us the Spirit as the first installment of his kingdom—as a down payment, earnest money (see 2 Corinthians 1:22). By his Spirit, the Lord of the kingdom already lives in us.

Paul hopes for the kingdom, but that doesn't mean he relishes the prospect of death. He does not look forward to the ultimate breakdown of earthly life, the parting of body and soul. Death is a dreadful thing. Paul wants his mortal life not to disintegrate but to be healed. He wants everything in himself that is subject to deterioration to be grasped by the divine power that will sustain him in life forever. He wants "what is mortal" to "be swallowed up by life" (2 Corinthians 5:4). And he knows that cannot happen in this present life, but only in God's kingdom to come.

Paul speaks of our present life, with its vulnerability to suffering and death, as life in a tent. Earthly life is like camping, Paul suggests—a temporary mode of existence. In Christ, death will be the end of our camping in the wilderness and our arrival at our homestead in the promised land.

The Spirit enables us to embrace this hope (see 2 Corinthians 5:5).

Understand!

1. Paul says that the Spirit in us is like a treasure stored in "earthen vessels"—in clay pots (2 Corinthians 4:7). What does he mean? How did Paul experience the truth of this statement in his own life and ministry?

_____

_____

_____

_____

_____

_____

2. What does it mean to carry in our body the death of Jesus (see 2 Corinthians 4:10)? In what way have you ever experienced this reality? How did it help to make manifest the life of Jesus in you (4:11)?

_____

_____

_____

_____

_____

_____

_____

3. Twice Paul writes, "We do not lose heart" (2 Corinthians 4:1, 16). What is it to lose heart? How does it happen? Is there anything in what Paul says here that could help a person to not lose heart?

_____

_____

_____

_____

_____

_____

4. Paul terms the sufferings of this present life a "slight momentary affliction" (2 Corinthians 4:17). Yet he also says that he is _always_ being given up to _death_ for Jesus' sake (see 4:11), which sounds serious. How can afflictions that are lifelong and heavy be momentary and slight?

_____

_____

_____

_____

_____

5. How would you respond to someone who says that Paul seems to regard earthly life as unimportant or undesirable (see 2 Corinthians 4:17–5:5)?

_____

_____

_____

_____

_____

_____

▶ In the Spotlight
Not a Stoic

Some people's approach to suffering is that you should just learn to endure it. As much as possible, you shouldn't let problems or pain bother you. A strong person doesn't let suffering get him down but keeps on going in any situation.

Some people think this is the Christian approach to suffering. Actually, it is closer to an ancient philosophical outlook called Stoicism. Stoicism was popular at the time of St. Paul. But St. Paul's approach to suffering is different from that of the Stoics.

According to biblical scholar Victor Paul Furnish, the Stoics talked about holding on to your tranquility in the midst of adversity and even of making yourself "invincible" in the face of hardships. But, Furnish points out, Paul speaks of being comforted in his afflictions (see 2 Corinthians 1:4-7; 7:6-7, 13) and even of being rescued from them (2 Corinthians 1:10). Furnish compares St. Paul's attitude to suffering to that of the Stoic Epictetus:

The distinctiveness of the Pauline perspective on suffering is vividly exhibited when the opening sentence of Epictetus' discourse on struggling against difficulties . . . is put alongside 2 Corinthians 4:7-9. For Epictetus, "It is difficulties that show what men are" . . . because difficulties must be met and overcome with the disciplined power of reason and with courage. For Paul, however, difficulties must be met and borne with faith, and thereby they disclose not "what men are" but *that the power which is beyond any comparison belongs to God and not to us.*

For Paul, suffering is not an opportunity to show how strong we are but an opportunity to trust God and to see how strong God is. This is not to say that Christians should be weak in the face of suffering. Paul himself was courageous (see 2 Corinthians 12:1-10). But his strength was based on trust in God.

Grow!

1. St. Paul says, "Where the Spirit of the Lord is, there is freedom" (2 Corinthians 3:17). What freedom has the Spirit brought into your life? What freedom do you still need him to bring? How can you cooperate with his liberating you?

_____

_____

_____

_____

_____

_____

_____

2. Reread 2 Corinthians 3:17-18; 4:6. What helps you to behold the face of Christ? Looking at an icon of him? Gazing at a painting or sculpture? Picturing a gospel scene in your mind? Simply being quiet before the Blessed Sacrament? Some other way? How might you make more use of this means of looking at Jesus?

_____

_____

_____

_____

_____

_____

3. In what way, large or small, have you experienced the Spirit changing you to be more like Jesus? In what area of your life would you especially like him to change you now? From your experience of the Spirit's help in the past, what can you learn that would help you cooperate with the Spirit's action in this area of your life?

_____

_____

_____

_____

_____

_____

4. Think of a situation in which good came from suffering, either in your own life or the life of someone you know. What can you learn from this about the ways God may act in our lives? Is there something in this session's reading that speaks to you in some way about a painful area of your life?

_____

_____

_____

_____

_____

_____

_____

5. In what circumstances do you tend to become discouraged? Why?
Is there something in this session's reading that could help you
overcome discouragement in that situation? Is there a change in
your thinking or a decision you need to make that would give
you hope?

_____

_____

_____

_____

_____

_____

▶ In the Spotlight
We Share Christ's Suffering in Our Work

*Not only missionary work, like Paul's, but all work can be a
sharing in Jesus' sufferings on behalf of others. In his 1981
encyclical* Laborem Exercens (On Human Work), *Pope John
Paul II wrote:*

Sweat and toil, which work necessarily involves in the present
condition of the human race, present the Christian and everyone who is called to follow Christ with the possibility of sharing lovingly in the work that Christ came to do. This work of
salvation came about through suffering and death on a Cross.
By enduring the toil of work in union with Christ crucified
for us, man in a way collaborates with the Son of God for the

redemption of humanity. He shows himself a true disciple of Christ by carrying the cross in his turn every day in the activity that he is called upon to perform.

—**Pope John Paul II,** *Laborem Exercises*

Reflect!

1. Paul says that we don't become more and more like Christ from our own resources, but from the Spirit living in us (2 Corinthians 3:18). The Spirit uses many aids to bring about our transformation—from prayer and study (the liturgy and the sacraments, Scripture, accounts of saints) to opportunities for action (jobs, families, social responsibilities, friendships). What means is the Spirit using especially in your life at present? How could you better cooperate with him?

2. Reflect on these New Testament passages (the words of Paul, James, and Jesus), which speak about the Holy Spirit's presence in us and about seeking more of the presence of the Spirit.

> If the Spirit of him who raised Jesus from the dead dwells in you, he who raised Christ Jesus from the dead will give life to your mortal bodies also through his Spirit which dwells in you. . . .
>
> We know that the whole creation has been groaning in travail together until now; and not only the creation, but we ourselves, who have the first fruits of the Spirit, groan inwardly as we wait for adoption as sons, the redemption of our bodies. For in this hope we are saved. Now hope that is seen is not hope. For who hopes for what he sees? But if we hope for what we do not see, we wait for it with patience.

Likewise the Spirit helps us in our weakness; for we do not know how to pray as we ought, but the Spirit himself intercedes for us with sighs too deep for words. And he who searches the hearts of men knows what is the mind of the Spirit, because the Spirit intercedes for the saints according to the will of God.

—Romans 8:11, 22–27

Count it all joy, my brethren, when you meet various trials, for you know that the testing of your faith produces steadfastness. And let steadfastness have its full effect, that you may be perfect and complete, lacking in nothing.

If any of you lacks wisdom, let him ask God, who gives to all men generously and without reproaching, and it will be given him. . . .

Every good endowment and every perfect gift is from above, coming down from the Father of lights with whom there is no variation or shadow due to change.

—James 1:2-5, 17

And I tell you, Ask, and it will be given you; seek, and you will find; knock, and it will be opened to you. For every one who asks receives, and he who seeks finds, and to him who knocks it will be opened. What father among you, if his son asks for a fish, will instead of a fish give him a serpent; or if he asks for an egg, will give him a scorpion? If you then, who are evil, know how to give good gifts to your children, how much more will the heavenly Father give the Holy Spirit to those who ask him!

—Luke 11:9-13

▶ In the Spotlight
Just Looking . . . and Looking

This is a story about St. John Vianney, a nineteenth-century pastor, or "curé," of the village of Ars, France.

Each evening as night was falling, the Curé of Ars saw a field laborer enter his country church. He remained there a long time, his lips not moving.

After observing him a while, the intrigued Curé asked him, "What do you do here?"

"Why, I pray to Jesus."

"And what do you say to him in your prayer?"

"I say nothing to him; I look at him and he looks at me!"

This man had received no instruction from any human master. He had read no theological treatise; he was ignorant of the ways of prayer. However, he had been instructed by the Holy Spirit, and the Spirit had revealed to him this method of prayer. He knew that the best prayer was a simple exchange of "looks" between God and the soul. Such a look said everything because it came from the heart, and the heart does not need words. The heart communicates with a single glance.

—**Lucien-Louis Bunel,** from *Père Jacques: Resplendent in Victory*

Act!

Identify an area of your life in which you experience sorrow or discouragement. Take the next week (or nine days—the classic length of time for a novena), and bring your sorrow and discouragement to God in prayer each day. In addition, ask God to give you more of his Holy Spirit. End each time of prayer with the Our Father.

▶ In the Spotlight
The True Light

We have seen the true light; we have received the heavenly Spirit;
we have found the true faith; and we worship the undivided
Trinity, for the Trinity has saved us.
—**Byzantine Liturgy, Prayer after Communion**

Through the Holy Spirit we are restored to paradise, led back
to the Kingdom of heaven, and adopted as children, given confidence to call God "Father" and to share in Christ's grace, called
children of light and given a share in eternal glory.
—**St. Basil the Great**

Heavenly King, Comforter, Spirit of Truth,
everywhere present and filling all things,
Treasury of blessing and Giver of Life,
come and dwell within us,
cleanse us of all stain,
and save our souls,
O gracious One.
—**Byzantine Hymn**

Practical Pointers for Bible Discussion Groups

Bible discussion group is another key that can help us unlock God's word. Participating in a discussion or study group—whether through a parish, a prayer group, or a neighborhood—offers us the opportunity to grow not only in our love for God's word but also in our love for one another. We don't have to be trained Scripture scholars to benefit from discussing and studying the Bible together. Bible study groups provide environments in which we can worship and pray together and strengthen our relationships with other Christians. The following guidelines can help a group get started and run smoothly.

Getting Started

- Decide on a regular time and place to meet. Meeting on a regular basis allows the group to maintain continuity without losing momentum from the previous discussion.

- Set a time limit for each session. An hour and a half is a reasonable length of time in which to have a rewarding discussion on the material contained in each of the sessions in this guide. However, the group may find that a longer time is even more advantageous. If it is necessary to limit the meeting to an hour, select sections of the material that are of greatest interest to the group.

- Designate a moderator or facilitator to lead the discussions and keep the meetings on schedule. This person's role is to help preserve good group dynamics by keeping the discussion on track. He or she should help ensure that no one monopolizes the session and that each person—including the shyest or quietest individual—is offered an opportunity to speak. The group may want to ask members to take turns moderating the sessions.

- Provide enough copies of the study guide for each member of the group, and ask everyone to bring a Bible to the meetings. Each session's Scripture text and related passages for reflection are printed in full in the guides, but you will find that a Bible is helpful for looking up other passages and cross-references. The translation provided in this guide is the Revised Standard Version (Catholic Edition). You may also want to refer to other translations—for example, the New American Bible or the New Jerusalem Bible—to gain additional insights into the text.

- Try to stay faithful to your commitment and attend as many sessions as possible. Not only does regular participation provide coherence and consistency to the group discussions, but it also demonstrates that members value one another and are committed to sharing their lives with one another.

Session Dynamics

- Read the material for each session in advance, and take time to consider the questions and your answers to them. The single most important key to any successful Bible study is having everyone prepared to participate.

- As a courtesy to all members of your group, try to begin and end each session on schedule. Being prompt respects the other commitments of the members and allows enough time for discussion. If the group still has more to discuss at the end of the allotted time, consider continuing the discussion at the next meeting.

- Open the sessions with prayer. A different person could have the responsibility of leading the opening prayer at each session. The prayer could be a spontaneous one, a traditional prayer such as the Our Father, or one that relates to the topic of that particular meeting. The members of the group might also want to begin some of the meetings with a song or hymn. Whatever you choose, ask the Holy Spirit to guide your discussion and study of the Scripture text presented in that session.

- Contribute actively to the discussion. Let the members of the group get to know you, but try to stick to the topic so that you won't divert the discussion from its purpose. And resist the temptation to monopolize the conversation, so that everyone will have an opportunity to learn from one another.

- Listen attentively to everyone in the group. Show respect for the other members and their contributions. Encourage, support, and affirm them as they share. Remember that many questions have more than one answer and that the experience of everyone in the group can be enriched by considering a variety of viewpoints.

- If you disagree with someone's observation or answer to a question, do so gently and respectfully, in a way that shows that you value the person who made the comment, and then explain your own point of view. For example, rather than saying, "You're wrong!" or "That's ridiculous!" try something like "I think I see what you're getting at, but I think that Jesus was saying something different in this passage." Be careful to avoid sounding aggressive or argumentative. Then watch to see how the subsequent discussion unfolds. Who knows? You may come away with a new and deeper perspective.

- Don't be afraid of pauses and reflective moments of silence during the session. People may need some time to think about a question before putting their thoughts into words.

- Maintain and respect confidentiality within the group. Safeguard the privacy and dignity of each member by not repeating what has been shared during the discussion session unless you have been given permission to do so. Then everyone will get the greatest benefit out of the group by feeling comfortable enough to share on a deep and personal level.

- End the session with prayer. Thank God for what you have learned through the discussion, and ask him to help you integrate it into your life.

The Lord blesses all our efforts to come closer to him. As you spend time preparing for and meeting with your small group, be confident in the knowledge that Christ will fill you with wisdom, insight, grace, and the ability to see him at work in your daily life.

Sources and Acknowledgments

SESSION 1: A JOYFUL VISIT

Byzantine Hymn, Mother Mary and Archimandrite Kallistos Ware, trans., *The Festal Menaion* (London: Faber and Faber, 1969), 454.

Bede, *Homilies on the Gospels,* 4.1; adapted from *Homilies on the Gospels,* Lawrence T. Martin and David Hurst, OSB, trans., Cistercian Studies, vol. 110 (Kalamazoo, MI: Cistercian Publications, 1991 and 1993).

Origen, *Homilies on St. Luke*, trans. by Kevin Perrotta.

Maximus of Turin, in Arthur A. Just., Jr., *Luke, Ancient Christian Commentary on Scripture*, New Testament, vol. 3 (Downers Grove, IL: InterVarsity Press, 2003), 21.

SESSION 2: AN UNEXPECTED MEETING

St. Frances Cabrini, *The Travels of Mother Frances Xavier Cabrini*, as related in several of her letters (Exeter: Giovanni Serpentilli, 1925).

St. Francis de Sales, *Treatise on the Love of God*, H. B. Mackey, OSB, trans. (Westminster, MD: The Newman Bookshop, 1942), 340–42.

Session 3: Jesus Challenges His Neighbors

St. Anthony of Egypt, "Directions on Life in Christ," in E. Kadloubovsky and G. E. H. Palmer, trans. and eds., *Early Fathers from the Philokalia* (London: Faber and Faber, 1954), 45–46.

Witness of Anne from Canada taken from *When the Spirit Speaks*, Peter and Debbie Herbeck (Cincinnati: Servant Books, 2007), 109–11. Used with permission of the authors.

Session 4: Roaming in the Spirit

St. Frances Cabrini, *The Travels of Mother Frances Xavier Cabrini*, as related in several of her letters (Exeter: Giovanni Serpentilli, 1925).

Blessed Columba Marmion, *The English Letters of Columba Marmion, 1858–1923*, G. Ghysens and T. Delforge, eds. (Baltimore and Dublin: Helicon, 1962), 141.

Session 5: Blooming in the Spirit

Witness of Deanna from Michigan taken from *When the Spirit Speaks*, Peter and Debbie Herbeck (Cincinnati: Servant Books, 2007), 54–55. Used with permission of the authors.

St. Francis de Sales, *Treatise on the Love of God*, H. B. Mackey, OSB, trans. (Westminster, MD: The Newman Bookshop, 1942).

David Mangan, *God Loves You and There's Nothing You Can Do About It: Saying Yes to the Holy Spirit* (Cincinnati: Servant Books, 2008), 87–88. Reprinted with permission of St. Anthony Messenger Press, 28 W. Liberty St., Cincinnati, OH 45202

Session 6: Looking at Jesus

Blessed Columba Marmion, *The English Letters of Columba Marmion, 1858–1923*, G. Ghysens and T. Delforge, eds. (Baltimore and Dublin: Helicon, 1962), 128.

Ralph P. Martin, *2 Corinthians:* Word Biblical Commentary, vol. 40 (Nashville: Thomas Nelson, 1986), 82.

Victor Paul Furnish, *II Corinthians:* Anchor Bible, vol. 32A (Garden City, NY: Doubleday, 1984), 282.

Pope John Paul II, Encyclical Letter: *Laborem Exercens*, 27.3, issued September 14, 1981, accessed at www.vatican.va.

Lucien-Louis Bunel in *Père Jacques: Resplendent in Victory*, Francis J. Murphy (Washington, DC: ICS Publications, 1998), 165.

St. Basil the Great, *On the Holy Spirit,* 15, 36, quoted in the *Catechism of the Catholic Church*, 736.

Also in The Word Among Us Keys to the Bible Series

Jesus' Journey to the Cross: A Love unto Death

Accompany Jesus through the events of his passion, death, and resurrection. Six sessions feature commentary and questions for reflection and discussion as well as wisdom from the saints, contemporary stories of faith, and fascinating historical background. Item# BTWGE9

Treasures Uncovered: The Parables of Jesus

This popular six-session Scripture guide will help you explore the surprising—and often challenging—dimensions of six of Jesus' parables. Fascinating historical details, explanations of the Greek root words used in the original gospels, and quotations from Church fathers included. Item# BTWAE5

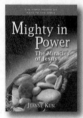

Mighty in Power: The Miracles of Jesus

This Scripture guide will help you understand the miracles of Jesus as invitations to experience God's mercy and salvation today. Each of the six sessions includes questions for delving into the miracles of Jesus and applying them to daily life. Suitable for individuals or groups. Item# BTWBE6

Food from Heaven: The Eucharist in Scripture

Food from Heaven will help you understand and appreciate the biblical foundations of the Mass, and especially of the Eucharist. Among the passages studied are Old Testament stories that foreshadow the Eucharist, along with gospel scenes that bring Jesus' own teaching to life. Item# BTWCE7

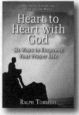

Heart to Heart with God

Heartfelt prayer is effective! This Bible study guide explores six attitudes or actions that will bring passion to your prayer. Author Deacon Ralph Torrelli encourages prayer that is persistent, bold, expectant, and specific, and includes real-life testimonies of God's amazing responses to such prayers. Item# BTWEE8

To order call 1-800-775-9673 or order online at wau.org